LOVE in the AIR
Second World War Letters

by Joanne Culley
with selections from letters by
Harry Culley and Helen Reeder

FriesenPress

Suite 300 - 990 Fort St
Victoria, BC, Canada, V8V 3K2
www.friesenpress.com

Library and Archives Canada Cataloguing in Publication

Culley, Joanne, author Love in the air : Second World War letters / by Joanne Culley.

Includes bibliographical references. Issued in print and electronic
formats. ISBN 978-1-4602-6226-9 (bound). --ISBN 978-1-
4602-6227-6 (pbk.). --ISBN 978-1-4602-6228-3 (pdf)

1. Culley, Harry, 1914-2009--Correspondence. 2. Reeder, Helen,
1919-1997--Correspondence. 3. Canada. Royal Canadian Air Force. Concert Band--
Biography. 4. Canada. Department of Munitions and Supply--Officials and employees-
-Biography. 5. World War, 1939-1945--Personal narratives, Canadian. I. Title.

D811.5.C84 2015 940.54'8171 C2015-900820-4 C2015-900879-4

ISBN
978-1-4602-6226-9 (Hardcover)
978-1-4602-6227-6 (Paperback)
978-1-4602-6228-3 (eBook)

1. Biography & Autobiography, Personal Memoirs

Distributed to the trade by The Ingram Book Company

Table of Contents

To my parents, whose love endured

Introduction

When I was young, my mother would sometimes get a dreamy look in her eyes and say, "Your father and I were apart for close to three years during the Second World War, but we wrote to each other almost every other day." When I'd ask to see the letters, she would get out the dusty old Eaton's box and let me look at them, but she wouldn't let me read them. She told me they were private and spoke of a deep love she hoped I would also experience one day.

While clearing out their house after my father's death (my mother had died twelve years earlier), I came upon that same box in the bottom dresser drawer. Not knowing what to do with it, I took it home and stowed it away in my closet. I didn't want to break the confidence of the parents I had loved so much, and who had loved each other. But how could I discard those letters, unread?

Ultimately, curiosity got the better of me. Looking inside, I found several neatly stacked bundles of blue airmail letters, tied with yellow ribbons, and a note saying, "Letters written from 1943 to 1946 between Harry and Helen." I took this as permission to delve further.

There were 609 letters from each to the other—quite rare for both sides of a correspondence from that time to survive. I wasn't surprised that my mother had kept those he sent to her, but I was amazed that my father had carried all of her letters with him in his kit bag, while he travelled around the British Isles during the war. As I read through them, I discovered not just declarations of undying love, but also detailed descriptions of what was happening on both sides of the Atlantic.

When Canada declared war on Nazi Germany in September 1939, many Canadians joined the war effort, anxious for work and a place to live after enduring the long, hard years of the Great Depression. The Canadian economy went into full swing, with factories making airplanes, tanks, ships, and munitions.

The first years of the war were not good for the Allied nations, which included the United Kingdom, France, Poland, Canada, and other British Commonwealth countries. Germany had taken over most of Europe—Poland, Denmark, Norway, the Netherlands, Belgium, and France. Britain was next on the list, and in 1940, the Battle of Britain began, with German planes making air assaults on English cities, especially London, in what became known as "the Blitz." In August 1942, Allied troops, predominantly Canadian, attempted an invasion of Europe through the French coastal town of Dieppe, with devastating results: more than half the soldiers, about 3,600, either died or were taken prisoner.

With many of the men in the services, there was a shortage of workers in offices and manufacturing plants. Thousands of Canadian women rose to the challenge of filling those jobs, moving from farms and small towns to larger centres.

Helen Reeder was the eldest daughter of eleven children growing up in an impoverished Saskatchewan farm family during the Depression. Seeing no future for herself there, she studied shorthand and typing through correspondence courses and at a secretarial school. When she was twenty-two, she found a job in Ottawa in 1942 working as a secretary at the Department of Munitions and Supply, then later as a cashier and stenographer at the Toronto Transportation Commission, as it was then known.

Like many Canadians, Harry Culley from Toronto wanted to make a contribution. He joined up in early 1942 at the age of twenty-seven to be part of the Royal Canadian Air Force No. 3 Personnel Reception Centre Band, one of five bands that went overseas. During the Depression, he had had difficulty finding steady work. After finishing high school in 1931, he had taken a number of odd jobs: working as a bookkeeper at a wholesale tobacconist, as a shoe salesman at Eaton's in Toronto, and as a musician, his first love, playing clarinet and saxophone. There was a tradition of music in his family; his great-grandfather Teck Culley had played flute in the Toronto Symphony Orchestra, and his parents Harry Culley Sr. and Ida Culley (stage name Claudette) were a popular piano duo, playing on stage and on the radio. But Harry Jr. had had a hard time establishing himself as a musician, as band work was sporadic. He played at dances in the Deseronto area of Ontario, worked at the Royal Hotel in Honey Harbour during the summers, and played in a trio at the Savarin Restaurant in Toronto. When he passed the performance and theory tests required to be part of an RCAF band, he was offered a steady pay cheque and the opportunity to be a full-time musician. After enlisting, he was sent to Ottawa for training at the RCAF Station Rockcliffe.

If it had not been for the war, the two likely would never have encountered each other. It was in Ottawa where Helen and Harry met, dated and became engaged prior to his leaving for overseas.

Throughout the war, the RCAF's five bands and a dance band played in approximately 3,000 concerts, dances, and parades as well as making recordings for the BBC. While there, Harry endured bombings in London, the overall scarcity of food, and the exhaustion of travelling by trains, buses, and army trucks with irregular schedules. But he and the other band members knew that their music was keeping up the morale of soldiers and civilians alike, especially during the dark early years of the war.

During their two and a half years apart, Harry and Helen kept their love alive through letters and packages: She sent over care boxes filled with cookies, fruitcakes, and candies, as well as homemade items such as woollen socks and scarves. And he sent her flowers and jewellery for her birthday, Valentine's Day, and Christmas.

Deciding which of the letters to include was a challenging process. I selected excerpts from some of the more interesting letters and composed imagined scenes inspired by the content of other letters, to provide a context for what was happening in both of their lives. I have tried to place the letters as closely as possible by date, to show the couple responding to each other's questions and comments. However, because of delays in the delivery of letters on both sides, especially around the time of D-Day, often neither Harry nor Helen received a letter from the other for several weeks. Occasionally, I have grouped the letters thematically, as opposed to chronologically, so that the narrative flows more smoothly.

Of their love letters, Helen wrote, "We'll bind them up and read them over about twenty years from now. . . . It's a nice thought." I don't think they ever did sit down together to re-read those letters—they were too busy living the lives they had dreamed about all those years before.

I

Love Blooms

The evening breeze caressed the trees tenderly
The trembling trees embraced the breeze tenderly
Then you and I came wandering by
And lost in a sigh were we

"Tenderly," lyrics by Jack Lawrence, music by Walter Gross

In early September 1942, a bus pulled into the Royal Canadian
Air Force Station Rockcliffe about four miles northeast of the
Parliament Buildings in Ottawa carrying members of the RCAF
No. 3 Personnel Reception Centre Band. Out the windows they
could see the airfield, where planes of all sizes and purposes
were parked or flying in and out—mail transport carriers, pas-
senger planes, bombers, and even floatplanes were landing at
the dock on the Ottawa River. Surrounding the fields was an
assortment of hangars, barracks, and other buildings.

Steve, the bandmaster, made some announcements before
they got off the bus.

"We've been assigned to Barracks B on the upper cliff, and
the mess hall is just a little farther east along the river," he said.
"The hangars and runways are on the ground level."

"I guess that's why they call it Rockcliffe," whispered Ossie to Harry. The two clarinetists sat beside each other in the band.

"You'll start basic training tomorrow morning: first-aid, drill, ceremonial, and small-arms handling," continued Steve. "Meanwhile, you can unpack and get out your instruments, as we have a rehearsal in one hour to prepare for our performances during the next few days—at Major's Hill Park tomorrow and Parliament Hill on Friday afternoon. The dance band plays at the Red Triangle Club that night."

"What in the devil is the Red Triangle Club?" Harry wondered under his breath.

"I have no idea, but I guess we'll find out soon enough," said Al Smith, nicknamed Smitty, who played French horn in the concert band and piano in the dance band.

"I'm sure I don't need to tell you this, but just remember we are all part of the military effort and are considered a valuable resource for the Allies, so don't let anyone make you feel inferior because you're in a non-combat job[1]—we all have a role to play to keep up morale and win this war," said Steve.

At that, everyone cheered.

Entering the barracks, the band members laid their kit bags down on their bunk beds. It had been a long day, taking the train from Toronto, then the bus from Union Station at the Chateau Laurier Hotel.

Smitty grabbed the bunk above Harry and got out his book.

"What are you reading?" Harry asked.

"*The Thin Man* by Dashiell Hammett—I've got to find out who did it."

"Well, that's one way to escape," Harry said, looking out the window down to the airfield below, where he could see some

---

1   Many of the non-combatant military personnel expressed guilt at not fighting the enemy directly. In fact, the percentage of those in support positions, such as musicians, secretaries, mechanics, drivers, cooks, canteen workers, clerks, administrative workers, doctors, nurses, and more, was approximately 60 percent, exceeding the percentage of combat personnel, which was at 40 percent.

wounded air force personnel being removed on stretchers from a plane. "I'm wondering what it'll be like over there."

"Best not to think about it," Smitty said. "No sense worrying about something we can't do anything about."

"It's hard to ignore the papers," Harry said, unpacking the *Toronto Telegram* from his bag and reading, "'Liverpool Endures Seventh Night of Raids by Luftwaffe: After a week-long bombardment by the German air force, thousands are dead, with extensive damage to the docks and industrial buildings. . . .' Last month London was the target, now it's Liverpool—who knows where they will strike next? I do hope it settles down by the time we get there."

"I think it'll be a while before we're shipped out, from what Steve says. The No. 1 band is already over there, and I would imagine there's limited travel when the raids are going on."

"Yes, I think the last thing people want when the bombs are falling is to hear a band playing, unless they like that old saying, 'fiddling while Rome burns,'" Harry said, unpacking his gear.

"Best just to think one day at a time and enjoy every moment we've got. Who knows, we might even meet some girls here."

"Now you're dreaming."

* * *

The YMCA operated "Red Triangle" social clubs in several Canadian cities so that service personnel on the move could have some recreation before going overseas. The clubs were so named because of the YMCA's logo, an inverted red triangle with the words "mind, body, and spirit" on the sides. Volunteer hostesses welcomed members of the army, navy, and air force during the nightly entertainment, which usually consisted of a dance band, variety program, touring army show, or Victory Bond drive to raise much-needed capital for the war effort. Organizations, schools, church groups, and businesses threw their energy behind these drives, which raised about $12.5 billion over the six years of the war.

"The Red Triangle Club is in that wooden building over there," Eleanor said as she pointed across the street. "It used to be the badminton club. Every night there's a different group of men from all of the services—they're moved around so much while they're in training. Some are here only a day or two. Many of them are staying at the barracks in Rockcliffe."

"Where's that?" Helen asked. She was glad that her friend from Saskatchewan had moved to Ottawa a few months earlier and could show her around. They were both working at the new Department of Munitions and Supply.

"It's farther east along the river. They want us to make the transition easier for the boys; for some of them, it's their first time away from home, so make an effort to be a bit friendly."

"I'll try. I know how they feel. I'm kind of homesick myself, everything is so new and different," Helen sighed. "I only just arrived here a couple of days ago, remember?"

As they entered the building, they could hear excited voices and clanking dishes echoing around the room.

"So here's the tea, coffee, and ginger ale. Wow, look at all the sandwiches and cookies there are tonight. The hostess club has been busy," Eleanor said.

Helen looked around at the stylishly dressed volunteers with their beautifully coiffed hair. She would have to bring her wardrobe up a notch to fit in with this crowd, she thought. She felt self-conscious in the dress that she'd made back home from her father's old suit. As soon as she got her first pay cheque, she'd go shopping. She'd also ask Lois at work for some tips on what to do with her hair.

Eleanor glanced over at the musicians setting up.

"Oh good. It's the air force dance band—should be some swinging music, not like that polka group we had last week. Once we've been around a few times with the refreshments, we get fifteen minutes to dance, then we have to be back on duty. We all take turns. One night a week, we can come and just dance if we like," Eleanor said.

Joanne Culley

As the first few notes of "In the Mood" wafted through the room, several women went over to the dance floor. It wasn't long before the servicemen in their clean, pressed uniforms cut in and took them as partners. The energy level increased as couples fox-trotted and jitterbugged, their bodies twirling and heads bobbing like popcorn on a fire.

Eleanor and Helen went back to the kitchen to replenish their trays.

"Sales of the bonds are going pretty well," said Mrs. Gibson, one of the older women. "If we keep feeding them, they might be more inclined to part with their money."

"Yes, we need to raise as much as possible. Things aren't looking too good over there," said Eleanor as she grabbed a tray. "Especially with all the Canadians we lost at Dieppe. Helen, did you know that Henry Roberts from home died in that raid?"

"No, I didn't. His mother and sisters must be devastated," Helen said, lowering her head.

"I've been meaning to ask you, how are things with you and John?" Eleanor asked.

"We broke up. It was hard, but I knew I didn't want to spend my life there. And I was lucky to get out unscathed, if you catch my meaning," Helen said.

Eleanor nodded and looked away.

After half a dozen songs, the band took a break. One of the musicians was heading their way.

"Hello, ladies, could a fellow get something to drink? I think I'm going to dry up, it's so hot up there," he asked, pulling at his collar.

"Certainly—here's some ginger ale," Helen replied with a sweet smile.

"Thanks. Are you enjoying the music?"

"It's wonderful. I especially liked the last one, 'Begin the Beguine,'" she said. "We don't hear much live music like that back where I come from."

"Where's that?"

"Thaxted, Saskatchewan. A long way from here."

"No kidding. I'm from Toronto, and I thought that was far away. Welcome to Ontario." There was a moment's pause as the two exchanged a shy smile and glance. "Well, gotta get back." He placed the empty glass on the tray and with a kind nod turned to join his band mates onstage.

"He's certainly a handsome one," Eleanor whispered as she gave Helen a playful nudge. "I think he likes you."

"Oh, don't be silly, he just wanted a drink and happened to come this way."

"No, really, I could see how intently he was looking at you and smiling," Eleanor observed. "Just wait and see. Look, he's the one playing the clarinet. Doesn't he look like Clark Gable with his pencil-thin moustache and slightly greying hair? The trumpeter is more my style, though," she added.

"We're just country girls, why would those sophisticated guys go for us?"

"Oh, you never know. We can always dream, can't we?"

"All the good-looking guys are going overseas. Why does there have to be a war?" Helen complained.

"Kiddo, if it weren't for the war, we wouldn't have the jobs we have. We'd be back home working our fingers to the bone on the farm. Just look at us now—we have our own money and a place to live," Eleanor pointed out.

"You're right. Let's just enjoy the music. We'll bask in their mellow tones and fine-looking faces while we can."

"Listen, your clarinetist is playing a solo," Eleanor said.

"Oh, I love this one—'Tenderly'—and his tone is so clear, he sounds like Benny Goodman. He's very good," Helen replied.

After the song, Helen visited the powder room to refresh her lipstick. In the mirror she saw a skinny, brown-haired country girl who was going to have to overcome her shyness if she was ever going to become a glamorous city girl.

"Come on, let's dance!" Eleanor grabbed her hand when she came back to the room.

At the end of the evening, the musicians descended from the stage carrying their stands and instruments. The one Helen had served glanced at her, raised his eyebrows, and smiled. He was heading in her direction.

"What are you up to now?" he asked.

"Just going home, I guess."

"How about I walk you there?" he asked shyly.

"It's quite a ways from Rockcliffe."

"That's all right, I can take the bus back," he said, taking her arm and leading her out the door. "By the way, my name's Harry. What's yours?"

Helen Reeder, Ottawa, 1943

Harry Culley, Ottawa, 1943

* * *

Helen and Harry dated for close to a year, going to movies, for long walks in the Gatineau Hills north of Ottawa, and to Toronto to meet his parents, all the while falling deeply in love. They knew, however, that the time would come when he would have to leave for war duty. The word finally came in August 1943. Not wanting to lose her, Harry presented Helen with an engagement ring, which she accepted wholeheartedly on August 6 in Queen's Park in Toronto. The next day, they were both scheduled to leave on trains going in opposite directions: Harry to Halifax, where he and the band would travel overseas on a troop ship, and Helen to Saskatchewan, to visit her family.

The din of the crowds resonated through Toronto's cavernous Union Station. Helen gazed at the ornately patterned ceiling above, but could find no joy in its beauty.

Harry looked dashing in his RCAF uniform, his canvas sack bulging in his arms like a baby. Side by side they made their way through the crowds, looking for the gate for Helen's train, which would be the first to leave. Six hours later Harry's train was leaving for Halifax.

Helen felt really uncomfortable in her new high heels and snugly fitted suit with her tight girdle underneath. But she had wanted Harry to remember her as a fashionable working woman. Passersby couldn't help staring at the attractive couple, so distraught, with the reasons clear to all.

When they reached the platform, her train was waiting.

"It's so cruel that we're heading off in different directions. Why can't we be travelling together?" Harry asked, dropping his bag and taking her into his arms.

"We will one day, darling, please remember that." Tears streamed down Helen's cheeks.

"Please wait for me. We'll invite everyone to our wedding."

"Don't worry about me, honey. You're the one who'll be tempted by all those lonely English girls. There aren't any men left over there—or here, for that matter."

"Never fear about that. I only have eyes for you. And it won't be long, just you wait and see."

"Goodbye, my love. I'll miss you with all my heart."

"I will too. I promise to write every chance I get."

The loudspeaker boomed, "Five-fifteen p.m. train to Vancouver, leaving on Platform 5. All aboard."

"Bye, honey, I love you," Harry mumbled, kissing and hugging his sweetheart tightly. Both fought their tears.

Forlornly, Helen climbed aboard, finding a seat near a window. Opening it, she called out and reached down to Harry, who was standing below.

As the train began to move, he walked more quickly, and she couldn't help laughing and crying at the same time as he tried to keep pace. Eventually he had to drop her hand. Waving, she called out, "Don't forget about your bag on the platform!"

Harry ran until he could go no longer, his arms hanging loosely at his sides. He watched until the caboose disappeared into the distance, west through the Exhibition grounds. Slowly, he walked back to pick up his kit bag. The crowds were so thick, he couldn't see it at first, but then he spotted it near the entranceway. Heaving it onto his shoulders, he headed to the coffee shop for a smoke, to kill the time until his parents and grandmother would come to see him off.

* * *

Helen settled into her seat, looking out the window as the train sped north through the rugged rock-studded forests of the Canadian Shield, land so different from the prairies.

She had a hard time holding back her tears. What a whirlwind the last year had been—dating and dancing with Harry, suppers out, declarations of love, becoming engaged, and now a sad parting. Would he stay true to her? How long would the war last? Would he come back alive?

To distract herself, she thought about going home to Thaxted, Saskatchewan, showing off her ring to her girlfriends, and sharing with her mother and younger sisters all the details of her new life. She was bringing them some much-needed cash; her purse was laden with $50 in small bills she had been carefully squirreling away over the last year in the preserving jar in her bed-sitting room in Ottawa. It was a peace offering to her parents, to assuage her guilt at leaving them two years before with five of their eleven children still at home. She also brought her ration book for her mother to help boost their food supplies for the winter.

Helen now had a sense of her importance in the wider world. She felt she was really doing something for the war effort. Even though her job in Steel Control at the Department of Munitions and Supply was clerical — keeping track of the materials needed for the factories, along with typing and mailing the orders for the raw materials—it seemed that her small contribution, when combined with the work of everyone on both sides of the Atlantic, was helping to turn the tide of the war. Her department was handling orders not only from Canada but also from Britain, and supplying much-needed armouries. Things did look better for the Allies than they had even a year before.

She considered herself fortunate to have landed the job in Ottawa after writing the federal government exam. She was proud to work in the department where C. D. Howe was the minister and remembered that he was the engineer who designed most of the western grain elevators. She mused about how things were changing—so many more women were needed to work now with all of the men going overseas.

The rhythmic rattling of the train lulled her into a reverie. Every few hours there'd be a stop, and uniformed men would get on and off, some coming home on leave, others going to different postings. Helen's brothers, Ray, Murray, and Jim, had already joined up. At least they'd get to see the world, not like the gang of harvesters who had boarded the train near Thunder Bay—middle-aged men, whose wrinkled, sunburned faces reflected the time they'd spent outdoors.

Now Harry too was on his way over. Never in her wildest dreams had Helen ever imagined she would be engaged to such a sophisticated, talented fellow. She had made the right decision in refusing John Passmore, her boyfriend back home, who was destined to take over his father's farm. She'd had a close call with him and was very lucky she hadn't become pregnant. She had seen enough of the drudgery involved in farm work to know that it wasn't for her. She felt that she deserved more, refusing to settle for the life that her mother had.

She and Harry had had their passionate moments, but she wanted to be married before they consummated their love. She wasn't going to take any more chances—there was too much at stake. She couldn't risk having a baby when he was on his way overseas to an uncertain future. Throughout the year they'd dated, Harry had been a gentleman and seemed to feel the same way she did, stopping before they'd gone too far. But sex wasn't something they talked about openly.

Helen prayed that neither she nor Harry would lose the feeling each had for the other. Taking out the photo he'd given her before they parted, she felt his presence. Would he come back the same as when he went away? She didn't want him to get a different look in his eyes or for his moustache to grow any bigger. After kissing his picture, she dozed off to sleep.

* * *

"How are the crops this year, Dad?" Helen asked as she climbed into the old Ford Model T. Her father had driven into town to meet her.

"We could have used more rain this summer, but it was nowhere near as bad as in the thirties."

"How are you managing without the older boys?"

"It's tough, but Lloyd and Jack can do almost the full day's work of a man. I tried to talk Ray, Murray, and Jim out of signing up, but you know boys—always out for an adventure. And Earl comes back to help whenever I need him." Her oldest brother had left home to work in the logging camps of northern Saskatchewan.

Helen cried when she saw her mother coming down the steps of the old wooden farmhouse. With more wrinkles and her shoulders sagging farther down, her body told the tale of bearing and caring for eleven children.

"Oh, Helen, it's so good to see you. Don't you look beautiful! You're going to be a fine married lady, living in the big city." Louisa clasped Helen to her bosom.

"Yes, Mother, can you believe it? I still can't."

Helen's five younger brothers and sisters ran out to greet her and clamoured to see her ring.

After the initial excitement, Helen settled into the routine of farm life, spending the mornings baking bread, helping the children with their homework in the afternoons, churning the butter, and relieving her mother of whatever housework she could.

A few days after she arrived, Helen was reading quietly in her room when she heard Jean bounding up the stairs, breathlessly announcing the words on the top envelope of a stack of mail in her hands: "Miss Helen Reeder, Thaxted, Saskatchewan, Canada. You have two letters!" she said excitedly to her older sister.

"Oh, they're from Harry." Helen had been waiting, wondering if he would write. She tore open the first one.

Halifax, Nova Scotia, Aug. 9, 1943

My darling Helen,

Well, here I am in Halifax. We landed last night in the rain after a very tiresome trip. The train didn't leave until 12:30 but we got a seat alright and played poker for a couple of hours (I won 11 cents). It kept my mind busy and I didn't brood.

I hope you had a nice trip darling, anyway you had an air-conditioned car. We pulled down a double seat and made a bed for the three of us. It's a good trick but you can only do it on these old cars. I'm always thinking of you darling the way you looked Thursday night.

I certainly miss you terribly every day and whenever I'm by myself I think of those last two days. Every detail seems to stick in my mind and everything we talked about is as clear as though we were together only last night. It's frightening to think how far we are apart and how much farther we will be apart. My only regret is that we aren't married.

However, I guess it's all for the best honey. I can't express my feelings very well, but you know how deeply I love you Helen and always will. Thank God we have memories to look back on sweetheart. O! for one kiss!

I'll have to close for now, be sure and have a good time at home.

All my love darling, Harry.

"What does he say?" Jean, aged 15, was watching her intently, waiting for any morsel of information.

"Well, he got to Halifax all right, thank goodness," Helen sighed. "Now, leave me alone so I can read the second one in peace." As she pondered his words and thought about their last lingering kiss before she got on the train, a thrill coursed through her body. Oh, to have him near her again.

The second letter was dated two days later.

Halifax, Nova Scotia, Aug. 11, 1943

Dearest Helen,

How are you sweetheart? I'll be looking for a letter from you when you get home [to Ottawa] *Darling and do have a nice vacation, you deserve it. Don't worry about me because everything is fine here and well-organized.*

I guess the holidays [out west] *have gone rather fast for you, what with meeting old friends again and going to those wild barn dances. I know what they are because I've played them. Ottawa will seem pretty dull by comparison.*

Well, Darling, all I can think of is you. I guess you would say, 'There he is with too much time on his hands again.' I suppose you're right as we don't have very much to do. I am playing a dance tonight at the officers' mess for which I get paid, believe it or not. So things aren't too bad you see. The first couple of days down here were pretty grim, darling, but once you get over the shock I guess it's not too bad, is it?

I saw your brother Jim last night, Murray was out as usual. Jim sure is a nice fellow and reminded me of you honey. We don't go into town very often, as the rumour goes that there are so many tough sailors around that they gang up on the airmen.

We're just living from day to day here because we don't know when we'll be leaving for overseas. I hope you still think of me now and then sweetheart.

Seeing that I've started every paragraph with I, which is very bad letter writing, I'd better finish it up right to the end. . . . I'll try and get in another groove as you call it. Do they talk that language away out there too? . . .

I don't think I'll give you any reason to worry about me. You know me well enough to know that I'm sincere when I say that.

I don't want you to feel alone ever, darling. I know it will be harder for you than it will be for me this winter, but with your kind of faith I know it will work out for the best for us both.

The day you accepted the ring was the happiest day in my life darling. That park will always be our park won't it sweetheart. This has been the happiest year of my life. It seems as if I'd known you for a long long time darling, we used to get along so well together, thanks to your patient and forgiving nature. I know I'm very trying at times.

All my love angel, Harry.

Helen ran downstairs, her heart pounding, to tell her mother.

"Harry says that he saw Jim in Halifax, really likes him, and that Jim reminds him of me!"

"Well, that's a relief that they're both still safe," her mother said, wiping the flour off her hands and hanging up her apron.

"Yes, and amazing that they found each other in such a large place."

Louisa moved closer to her daughter and gently placed a hand on Helen's arm. "Helen, I think you should wait out the war here. We'd love your company, and you could help with the girls."

"But I have a job to go back to in Ottawa, remember?"

"You could make some money here, keeping house for Mrs. Brown down the road. And we're hoping to move closer to town in the fall so the girls can go to high school."

"Let's talk about it later," Helen replied with a sigh, looking away. "Right now I'm going to write Harry, so it can go in the mail today."

As she went back up the sloping wooden stairs, Helen thought about her mother's words. Moving home would mean giving up everything—her social life, the new image she was cultivating for herself with stylish clothes and makeup, and, most of all, the independence that came from earning her own money.

Thaxted, Saskatchewan, Aug. 21, 1943

Dearest Harry,

It was a lovely day here; we were in town this morning and Mother and I finished quilting the comforter this afternoon. I'll bring it back with me for my hope chest.

I saw the most beautiful sunset last night, and I just sat gazing at it, thinking of the time we waited three hours to see one and it disappointed us, but we had a nice time waiting anyway, didn't we?

I know I'm going to feel so much alone without seeing you every other night. I think I only told you once that I loved you, but you always knew, didn't you? Well, I still do and as long as you feel the same about me, I couldn't do anything else but wait for you to come back to me.

My brother wanted me to go to another dance last night, but I didn't. There happens to be two or three old boyfriends around here that I don't care for anymore. Therefore, I try to avoid them. I just think about you all the time anyway, and I can stay home and do that.

I hear the clatter of dishes, so I should go and make myself useful. Hope your Sunday isn't too lonesome. How I wish you could come up and see me!

Goodbye dear.

Yours with love, Helen

2
England

Don't know why there's no sun up in the sky
Stormy eather
Since my man and I ain't together
Keeps rainin' all the time

"Stormy Weather," lyrics by Ted Koehler,
music by Harold Arlen

Canadian troops were transported to Great Britain on what had been luxury liners before the war and were now outfitted for moving soldiers and supplies. Ships that had previously carried about 2,000 civilian passengers now carried as many as 16,000 military personnel and crew on a single voyage.

After waiting in Halifax for about two weeks, the RCAF No. 3 Personnel Reception Centre Band travelled overseas. The band was one of several that were part of the war effort. Their mission was to help keep up spirits by entertaining the troops, officers, and civilians at concerts, dances, and parades.

Harry tossed and turned on the tiny bottom bunk. The band members were stacked in tiers four high and three across in the empty swimming pool on the stern deck. On his left were snoring men, on his right were cold and mildewed tiles that smelled of the ocean. Earlier that day they had boarded the RMS *Queen Mary*. Now, there was not much luxury in evidence—the ship was so crammed with servicemen, Harry could hardly move or think. How could they pack in eight times the number of people it should carry? And the ship kept veering off course. It was all he could do not to throw up.

"Why are we zigzagging so much?" Harry whispered to Smitty, who was reading his book with a tiny flashlight across from him.

"I think we're dodging the Gerry subs, or at least trying to— it would be just our luck to get blown up at sea," Smitty said, flicking his cigarette ash as he calmly turned the page.

"You're always full of comforting remarks." Harry tried to settle back down.

"I heard the captain say they've taken out the ship's stabilizers to make room for more men," Smitty continued. "So that's probably contributing to our bumpy ride."

Their first day at sea had been a long one, and there would be at least three more before they'd reach Scotland.

The next day they had morning and afternoon rehearsals in the stateroom for an evening concert in the officers' mess. At least he had his old clarinet that had been sent up to him before they left Halifax. It was the one that his grandmother bought him from Eaton's for $50—the instrument that set him up as a working musician. It had a clearer, purer tone than the newer one that was the standard issue.

"C'mon guys, you can do better than that. Put a little more swing into it!" Their bandmaster Steve was pretty hard on them, considering that the rough waters made it difficult for them to hold their instruments, never mind play together in rhythm. "You know what Winston Churchill said: 'Bands are necessary for the war effort; we have to keep everyone's morale up by dancing.'"

When their practice was finally over, Harry rushed several levels below deck to the telegraph office. He knew he couldn't tell her much because of the censors, but he wanted Helen to know they were okay and finally on their way.

[CABLE]
SEPT 3 SANS ORIGINE[1]
CANADIAN NATIONAL TELEGRAM
MISS HELEN R.
ALL WELL AND SAFE WRITING ALL MY LOVE
HARRY CULLEY

On September 4, 1943, the RMS *Queen Mary* landed in Greenock, west of Glasgow in Scotland, where the band members stayed briefly in the barracks there along with other incoming Allied troops. Harry took the opportunity to write his first letter from overseas.

Greenock, Clyde, Scotland, Sept. 4, 1943

Dearest Helen,

Just a few lines to let you know that I'm well and am enjoying myself very much. I hope you received my cable and I also sent a post card. We are in a very beautiful city [Greenock] *as you will see if you get the card, but* [we] *do not expect to stay long here as we will be going to our own station* [Bournemouth] *to play. Everybody seems to think we'll be travelling, but are not sure yet.*

I certainly miss you honey, but I guess you must miss me even more, if possible. We are rehearsing like mad and we certainly need it. The boys are

---

1   "Without origine": As a military operation, their location could not be revealed.

*looking forward to hearing the brass bands over
here as they are the best in the world. Nearly every
time a plane goes by overhead, somebody is sure
to look up (while we are rehearsing) and find out
whether it's one of ours or one of theirs. Rather
interesting pastime when counting 16 bars rest.
However, darling they feed and lodge us well here
and we're having a good time, so that's the main
thing. Will be looking for a letter.*

All my love, Harry

After its overnight stay in Greenock, the band travelled to
Bournemouth, England, by train, a more than eight-hour trip
south. Located on the English Channel, Bournemouth was
home to the Allied air forces from Britain and the United
States, and housed approximately 12,000 Canadians over the
course of the war.

Allied air force fighter planes left from Hurn, a large airfield just outside the city, in bombing raids across the English
Channel to the continent.

Throughout the war, child evacuees, civil servants, and
residents also came to the seaside city to escape the bombings
in London. To accommodate the increase in population, many
hotels, guesthouses, and private homes were commandeered
for meeting spaces, mess halls, entertainment venues, and
overnight lodgings. The RCAF officers' mess was located in
their headquarters at the Royal Bath Hotel, a prominent land-
mark in the city.

In an effort to prevent potential enemy landings,
Bournemouth citizens had dismantled their famous pier and
cordoned off the eleven-mile-long beach with barbed wire.
In spite of their efforts, however, one of the most devastating
raids on the city occurred on May 23, 1943, before the band
arrived, when over twenty Luftwaffe planes hit the Central

and Metropole Hotels, resulting in the deaths of seventy-seven civilians and 131 servicemen, many of them Canadian.

Over the course of the Second World War in Bournemouth, a total of fifty-one air raids with 2,271 bombs resulted in the deaths of 168 civilians and 182 servicemen, as well as 507 injuries.[2]

Once they'd reached Bournemouth, Harry received a letter from Helen.

Ottawa, Ontario, Sept. 9, 1943

My Darling Harry,

Your long awaited cable came last night about 9:45 and it was so good to hear that you were well. I felt so happy. I suppose there were thousands of others ahead of you all sending word home. You likely have bigger line-ups than we have here. Your Mother will be relieved too, I'm expecting to hear from her any day now. It was funny, but last night every time the doorbell rang I seemed to think it would be for me. You never disappoint me for long, do you darling?

I hope you feel a bit settled. Have you had much to do yet? I suppose there are so many Canadians around that you almost feel as though you're back home. You want to tell me all you can about life over there, etc., and what you do with yourself. Have you seen any English lassies? I guess they are mostly in uniform, aren't they?

Robert Donnell [Harry's friend, the carilloneur] *played a program on the Peace Tower Carillon yesterday. The Russian Anthem "Internationale" was played for the first time in Canada. There is*

---

2   M.A. Edgington, *Bournemouth and the Second World War, 1939–1945*

to be a big Air Cadets parade on Sunday led by the Central Band. I don't expect I'll see it unless it comes down Bank Street, but if you were in it – well –

I won't forget our good times, there's always something reminding me of them and of you, sweetheart.

Goodbye now. Please take care of yourself, and we all hope you won't be away too long. Please write lots.

My love always, Helen xxx

* * *

Harry and fourteen other band members were being billeted at a private hotel near the centre of downtown Bournemouth.

The Atherstone Hotel was a three-storey brick house with dormer windows, located at 15 Tregonwell Road. The street was named after the founder of the city, Lewis Tregonwell, so Harry supposed the house had been there quite a while.

The hotel was just a five-minute walk to the Pavilion, a haven near the beach that offered entertainment for the airmen stationed nearby, and where the RCAF presented many variety shows.

The old hotel had certainly seen better days. Faded velvet curtains, closed because of the blackout, enclosed the small, stuffy drawing room. The servicemen were greeted warmly at the front desk by an elderly couple, Mr. and Mrs. Lewis, the proprietors.

"Welcome to Bournemouth, boys! We hope you will find our humble lodgings comfortable. I wish it weren't wartime so that you could see the full beauty of this lovely city. I'm afraid our nice, sandy beaches are all blocked by the barbed wire. Churchill's worried about invasion channel-side, so I guess we can't take any chances. There are tank traps all over the channel too. By the way, it's a shilling per hour for a gas heater, and six pence for a bath—just let us know what you need."

Smitty and Harry lugged their kit bags and instruments up to their room on the second floor.

"Wow, would you look at that big, fat, beautiful mattress," Smitty remarked as he sat down to test it out. "I get the left side."

"Well, I guess we've seen the last of barracks life," said Harry. "We'd better unpack our meagre belongings. We've got to be over for rehearsal before playing in the officers' mess at 8 p.m."

They each had a chest of drawers in which to stuff their underwear and socks, and they hung up their uniforms and overcoats in the huge wardrobe. Grabbing their instruments, they headed off down the road. Their fellow band members were awaiting their arrival in the rehearsal area.

"These damn reeds are like shingles—they keep squeaking at the worst times," Harry complained to Ossie, who played second clarinet next to him.

"I've got news for you—they *are* cut from shingles," Ossie whispered.

"I've asked my mother to send a dozen new ones, medium-to-hard strength, in the next parcel—they're impossible to get here for love or money."

"Tell her to send us some new sheet music too. I'm tired of faking through these choruses. We sound pretty sad."

"Okay, fellows, that'll do for now. Make sure you're at the mess hall no later than 7:45. We want to impress the officers with our talent, paltry as it is." Steve's sarcasm was hard to take sometimes.

Quickly packing up, Harry headed back to his room to start on a letter to Helen.

Harry Culley at Atherstone Hotel in Bournemouth

Bournemouth, Sept. 6 - 22, 1943 [excerpts]
Opened by Examiner 4093

Dearest Helen,

Just a few lines to let you know that I'm well and am enjoying my stay here. One can really relax as it's so great and sunny, in fact, you'd hardly realize there is a war on, even when Italy surrendered yesterday.[3] A lift operator whispered the news to me very confidentially on Wednesday as I was going up to Bobby's Restaurant, as if it was a military secret. I can't help but wish you were

---

3   On September 3, 1943, British and Canadian troops landed in Italy and an armistice was signed with the Allies in Sicily.

Joanne Culley

over here with me. It's such a terrific place even in war time. I can just imagine what it would be with the lights on again.

[Smitty] *was saying it would be perfect to come back here and retire in one of these towns, everything seems so peaceful and quiet. Until the bombs start dropping, of course.*

I'm getting on to the money quite well, better than I thought at first. It's hard for me to realize that I'm in England, even now. It's just things like traffic driving on the left hand side of the road, blackouts that are really black, ancient lochs, looking for non-existent restaurants selling non-existent hot-beefs and respectable ladies drawing and serving beer, which, by the way, is so weak as to be almost tasteless. But, taking the good with the bad, it still is a swell country and not half as beaten down as we used to think at home.

You are practically overwhelming me with mail, but I love it. I guess I get more mail than anybody in the band and they are starting to tease me too. I got your letters of the 11th and 14th at noon. I don't think you need to worry about me not getting them as Mr. Churchill has said that there hasn't been a ship sunk in the North Atlantic for four months.

We played a banquet last night and after the officers cleared out we made a dive on the tables. There were big baskets of grapes, pears, and apples and we really went to town. Grapes are about $4.43 a pound. I'm still waiting for your parcel darling, so those cookies had better be good.

The band is improving immensely. I think I am too. Playing first clarinet makes you feel more important anyway. In a band of that size you have to work pretty hard to hold up your end.

Well darling, I'll have to close for now. I am trying to write under a blackout lamp.

I think I'm the luckiest guy in the world to have you writing to me all the time.

All my love darling, Harry.

Royal Canadian Air Force No. 3 Personnel Reception Centre Band, Harry Culley, front row, third from left, Al Smith, second row, third from left

Even though Harry had been writing Helen regularly, she had not yet received any of his letters from Bournemouth. They might have been held up because they had to go through the censor, or may have been delayed by transportation difficulties.

Ottawa, Sept. 11 – 15, 1943 [excerpts]

Dearest Harry,

How are you, darling? I'm still watching the mailman; should get word after ten days – that means around Wednesday I hope!! Even though your cable only contains eight words it has been read and repeated a dozen times. . .

I'm still a bit homesick and wish sometimes I'd stayed nearby at Saskatoon or Regina, but hope I'll be glad I came back if I ever get settled. Guess I'll be leaving here about the middle of October, but have nothing definite in mind. [Helen is planning on moving to Toronto to be closer to Harry's family, as that is where they will be living when he returns.] *There were no vacancies at my boss's Toronto office but they may help me to get placed. Everything is just a chance anyway so guess I should show my initiative and go to it!*

What's the climate like there, Harry? Does it rain as much as here? It seems a bit like winter today; the wind is so cold. Hope it won't be as bad as last year. Remember the time we walked to the Elgin Theatre [in Ottawa] *and nearly froze to death? You can wear your earflaps as much as you wish this year darling; I won't be around to criticize! They didn't look as bad as I said they did anyway.*

I hope you are able to get around there and see things on your weekends. Saturday and Sunday always passed so quickly for us, even if we did just _kill time_ *together sometimes. I was happier then than I ever realized because you filled my life and there was nothing lacking at the present. Now there's a missing link and it's you, sweetheart, but at least I can feel close when I write and think about you.*

You should know nearly everything I do every day. Do you want me to keep on writing as often? I feel so unsettled these days Harry. I told you in my last letter that I intended to leave here and trust to luck, but I was talking it over with the manager and he said if I stay he'd try to get some-thing better for me. The only reason I want to go [i.e. move from Ottawa to Toronto] *is to be nearer your folks and I'd like that, but the few friends I have are here and I feel quite at home except that I miss you terribly. If everything worked out well there I'd be happy but if I wasn't satisfied I'd be wishing I had stayed. Would you be disappointed if I didn't go up for awhile at least?Darling, you must get so tired reading about my affairs, but I seem to have to tell you everything. I want you to tell me about your experiences too and what you think about, etc. etc. Everybody teases me about writing to you so often, but I say you may not receive all of them.*

How I wish I could talk to you! I'm a bit worried about things in general but will have to think them out for myself, then tell you about it.

I was just down to Lois' place [her co-worker] *and we took a couple of pictures of each other in the house just experimenting. When we get talking the time seems to fly. Both Jimmy's and your ears should be ringing when we get together!!! We ate at the Arcadia, then she went to church and I came home. I'm here alone but when I'm writing to you I don't mind so much.*

Joanne Culley

I listened to the symphony program [on the radio] *this afternoon; tried to pick out the pieces you would like. I enjoy them, but wish I could follow them and whistle like you used to do. You always sounded so contented when you did that. Charlie McCarthy* [ventriloquist Edgar Bergen's dummy puppet] *is on now; I don't think Fred Allen has started yet, at least I haven't heard his program.*

I hope you begin to receive my mail soon, Harry. Isn't it terrible to go on from day to day without any letters? Maybe you don't notice it as much as I do. When we used to enjoy ourselves so much, I kept thinking there might be a time when things would be a bit different – this is the time!

I see by the bulletin board that the biggest aerial assault in history has saved the bridgehead of Salerno for the Allies. There must be some terrific fighting going on there. Wonder when and where the end will be.

Love and kisses. Helen

3
Supplying the War Effort

When they begin the beguine
It brings back the sound of music so tender
It brings back a night of tropical splendour
It brings back a memory of green

"Begin the Beguine," by Cole Porter

The Department of Munitions and Supply in Ottawa was formed during the Second World War and at its peak employed approximately 5,000 people. Helen was one of the 3,000 who worked in several temporary buildings constructed specifically to accommodate the influx.

"Miss Reeder, I'm ready for you now." Mr. Lauson sprung to his feet and looked out at her from his corner office.

"Certainly, sir," Helen said as she grabbed her steno pad, ink bottle, pen, and blotting paper, and went to his office. Looking out the window, she could see the green roofs and light limestone of the Parliament Buildings.

"This letter is to Mr. Percy Nightingale, Manager, United States Steel Export Company, and the address should be in your files," he said.

Dear Mr. Nightingale,

Thank you for your shipment of last Wednesday, which arrived without incident.

Please send us another 50 tons of first-grade steel by rail, as soon as possible. Please inform of amount due, which will be wired to your offices. The brokerage papers will arrive by separate mail. Thank you in advance for your prompt attention to this order.

Yours sincerely,
John Lauson
Deputy Steel Controller
Department of Munitions and Supply
Ottawa, Canada

"When you're finished typing the letter, you can put it on my desk for me to sign, then send it out in today's mail. It's hard to keep up with the shell and grenade production. The fighting overseas is escalating every day."

"Yes, sir," Helen said as she got up to leave.

"Oh, and Miss Reeder, I just got word that your release has gone through. We're going to really miss you here. It's not everyone who can type sixty words a minute and write a hundred words a minute in shorthand with no mistakes."

"Oh, you're flattering me, sir, I'm sure you'll find another stenographer in no time. But, I'll be sad to leave here too; everyone has been so good to me."

"Don't forget to remind me to write a reference letter for you. Whoever you work for next will be lucky to have you."

"Thank you, sir."

As she left her office that night, Helen felt despondent, unsure that she was making the right decision in leaving Ottawa to move to Toronto. It required a great deal of faith in

Harry and their future together to leave her job and the friends she'd made to start anew in a different city.

Helen Reeder with managers, Department of
Munitions and Supply, Ottawa

She headed south along O'Connor and turned right at Frank Street. It usually took a little over twenty minutes if she walked briskly. She had saved quite a bit of money on bus fare over the past year, money she was sending back home to her family. As she walked, Helen remembered the letter from her father that had arrived the day before, pleading with her to come back home and help her mother, who wasn't in good health. It tore her apart to think of her mother and all the hard work she'd done over the years while raising eleven children during the Depression. She loved them all and wished that somehow she could be in two places at once.

To alleviate her guilt, she would continue to send them money out of her pay of $25 a week (equivalent to about $350 in today's currency), $5 of which went toward her weekly room and board at Mrs. Nesbitt's, another $2 for lunches at work, about $3 or $4 for clothes and other expenses, and $5 for her savings account, leaving about $10 a week to help her family out. They could buy more food so that her mother wouldn't have to make everything from scratch, and maybe they could even hire extra help. There were **always teenage girls around** needing work. Helen just couldn't face moving back there, considering how much better her life had become since she left.

Supper was just about ready when she got in the door.

"How was your day, Helen?" Mrs. Nesbitt asked, bustling around, setting the table for dinner.

"Fine, thanks, but I'm feeling pretty sad about leaving them all. Oh, and before I forget, I picked up my ration books today—here are the coupons for sugar, butter, coffee, and meat like you asked."

"Thanks, I'll use them tomorrow when I order the groceries. It'll be hard to find another boarder as thoughtful as you."

After supper, they all gathered around the RCA Victor radiola in the living room.

"Ever since the war started, there are such interesting programs on," said Mrs. Nesbitt.

"I think Harry's parents are playing piano tonight—the show should be starting any minute," Helen replied.

"Shh," Mrs. Nesbitt hushed, motioning to the others who were talking in the background. Eleanor, Mabel, and Dorrien had brought their knitting and were busy comparing patterns.

"Tonight our show is brought to you by Lucky Strikes, the official cigarette of the Royal Canadian Air Force," said the announcer. "Tonight, our duo piano team Harry and Claudette Culley will play for you 'Sapphire,' 'Begin the Beguine,' 'The Dream,' and Bing Crosby's latest hit, 'Sunday, Monday, or Always.' This lovely couple have been rehearsing in the studio all day to present their polished program to you."

"Her real name is Ida—she uses Claudette as her stage name," Helen whispered to Mrs. Nesbitt, feeling proud that she was going to be related to these famous people. Listening to the music, she wondered about her future and how she would fit into Harry's family, considering her humble upbringing on the farm.

"Thank you, Harry and Claudette, for those sweet sounds," said the announcer. "And now they would like to say a few words to their listeners."

"We want to send out our greetings to our two sons, Harry Jr. in the RCAF and Ross in the navy. Harry is now overseas, stationed in Bournemouth."

"Are they musicians too?" asked the announcer.

"Yes, Harry Jr. plays clarinet and saxophone in the RCAF No. 3 Personnel Reception Centre Band, and Ross plays trombone in the First Navy Band."

"Well, I'm sure they'll bring their swinging melodies to all of our troops in Canada and overseas. Thank you for your show tonight. Be sure to smoke Lucky Strikes, the smoothest taste ever. And now, here is the latest news: Allied forces continue their advance through Italy, following their landing at the beach at Salerno last month, supported by air attacks from Britain . . ."

Mrs. Nesbitt got up to turn down the volume.

"How exciting to hear Harry's parents on the radio," said Eleanor.

"Very impressive indeed," said Dorrien. "Have you heard from him lately?"

"Yes, I finally got a letter yesterday, after not having received one for a month."

"They were probably held up by the censors," said Mrs. Nesbitt. "They're pretty careful about what news gets out."

"Well, I guess I'll go up and write to him and my mother," said Helen.

"Don't forget there's a big Victory Loan dance at the Red Triangle tomorrow night; the ladies from the church and the hostess club are making the sandwiches in the afternoon. We'll need more volunteer servers than ever," said Mrs. Nesbitt.

"I'll be there. Are you going, Helen?" asked Eleanor.

"I guess so," she replied, although her heart wasn't in it. How could it be, now that Harry wasn't there to dance with?

Helen Reeder (middle) and Eleanor
McAusland (right), Ottawa, 1943

Ottawa, Oct. 16 – 24, 1943 [excerpts]

Darling Harry,

I wasn't going to write you until tomorrow, but I couldn't wait to tell you that I heard your Mother and Father's broadcast tonight at 7:15. I was so surprised when their names were announced and the program was marvellous. They played "Sapphire," "Begin the Beguine," one of Count Basie's swing tunes, "The Dreamer," and "Sunday, Monday or Always." They will probably tell you about it but I had to tell you too. Their style of playing seemed different from any I've heard.

I've had a couple of letters from firms in Toronto and they don't offer a position as good as here. Prospects aren't very good in any respect, but I'm

Joanne Culley

going [to Toronto] *anyway at 3 p.m. on Oct. 31st. I'll go through with it now.*

Thanks for the nice air mail received yesterday, written on October 16th*. There is always something in your letters to tell people, and I'm really getting an idea of what it's like there from the little interesting things you tell me. How I'd like to go up and put my arms around you sometime when you are pretending to be waiting for me! All we can do is dream about it – yes, I still dream about you once in awhile, but not quite as exciting as that night I told you about. My, but you have a good memory for "some" things. I hope there was some mail waiting for you as you expected. Yes, I forgive you if you don't answer promptly but oh I love to get them. I get so excited no kidding!*

There is limited space so can't ramble on tonight. Will try and write again before I leave [for Toronto] *darling – are you back home* [in Bournemouth] *now?*

My love always, Helen.

* * *

Though it was stationed in Bournemouth on the southern coast, the band was expected to travel all over England, Scotland and Wales, bringing music to the citizens and military personnel in towns, in cities, and on stations. A month after arriving, Harry and his bandmates began their first tour.

Glasgow, Scotland, Belgrove Hotel, Oct. 16, 1943

Dearest Helen,

Arrived up here from London early this morning after playing a dance at Linton-on-Ouse near York and expect to leave to-morrow night to go back to London for a week. We do most of our travelling at night but I guess that eases the traffic during the day.

Little boys seem to roam the streets in droves laying for us because they think we still have chewing gum and candy. The people here are very generous and helpful and can't do enough for you but it's very hard for us to understand what they say as they talk so fast and have such a brogue. The women carry their babies in large shawls wrapped completely around themselves and the baby. It almost makes my heart skip a beat when I see them making a grab for a street car just as it's pulling away. Believe me they have a terrific take off. I did it once and just made it. When I recovered my senses, Smitty was still standing on the corner waving like mad a half block back. I guess I told you about the women conductors: boy, do they have to be tough, especially on a Saturday night, it keeps them busy throwing drunks off the car.

You must know how much I miss you darling. If I could see you for only a little while. I like to imagine when I'm in Trafalgar Square that I'm waiting for you because they say it's like Times Square in New York – everybody at one time or another during their lifetime comes to Trafalgar Square.

Another fellow and I were puzzled about which street to follow home from Trafalgar Square in the blackout when we ran into Smitty and another bandsman so you see the odds aren't so big after all! Smitty keeps asking strangers the way downtown and it's so funny because it's really all downtown as we know it. I don't think I'll get lost anymore as I have a small map to consult and also the tubes are easy to travel on and are very direct.

Of course there's no heating until next month but we retire very early as a rule due to the blackout and poor light in our room. The old man lights a grate every night for us from about six to about eight in the lounge so it's quite comfortable there.

Well darling, I've rambled on as long as I can after a very tedious day so will close for now. I should write Mother tonight, but won't. Do you still dream of me? I think that's the sweetest thing you've told me.

All my love, Harry.

* * *

It was Helen's first time volunteering at the Red Triangle Club since Harry had left. She felt strange going there, a place that held so many memories of their time together. As she entered the kitchen to get a tray of soft drinks, she was greeted warmly.

"Oh, here she is, we were wondering when you'd come back, Helen. Let's see your ring," Mrs. Gibson said.

Embarrassed at the attention, Helen modestly held out her left hand to display her sparkling solitaire diamond. As Mrs. Gibson admired it, she thought of how glad she was to have such a tangible reminder of Harry.

Glancing around at the tables, she saw the same old crowd. Some of those men would never get shipped out, she thought. They seemed to be on permanent detail at Rockcliffe. It wasn't fair—why did Harry have to leave?

"Don't worry, dear, the war will be over soon, and he'll be back before you know it," Mrs. Gibson said reassuringly, having noted the sombre look on Helen's face. "After all, the Allies have taken Italy now, so it won't be long before the rest of Europe goes too. We're gaining ground."

Helen bit her lip to stop the tears, and hurried out with the tray. All she could think of was how handsome Harry had looked when he used to come up to the counter and ask her for a drink. They had enjoyed themselves so much here. Even then, in the back of her mind, she had known there'd be a time when things would be different. She realized that she couldn't enjoy herself without him.

At least there wasn't a dance band performing tonight; there was a series of musical numbers and skits. The RCAF Review's fifteen-piece orchestra was setting up. How she wished Harry was up there on the stage.

When Helen went back to the kitchen for refills, Eleanor said, "I hear you finally got your release from the civil service."

"Yes, it took a long time. At first they wouldn't let me go, because of staff shortages, but then after I put my request in writing, and went through an hour of questioning, they finally approved it. It seems that it's easier to get into the government than to get out."

"Why on earth are you leaving such a good job, Helen?" Mrs. Gibson had overheard the conversation.

"Before he left, Harry asked me to move to Toronto, so that I could get to know the city and his family better. That's where we'll be living when he returns."

"Well, we'll certainly miss you here, won't we, girls? Especially with the Victory Loan drive on." They all nodded.

Helen just wanted to crawl through a hole, she felt so sad. She returned to the main room.

The music was nice, but after the umpteenth corny skit, and refusing several offers to dance with the Rockcliffe servicemen, she decided to go home. If she hurried, she could catch "Swing for the Services" on the radio. Then she would end her evening by writing Harry.

Ottawa, Oct. 1 - 19, 1943 [excerpts]

My Darling Harry,

We had a hectic night at the Triangle. We were so busy through the supper hour. The girls all tell me I'm different there now my eyes don't even rove around! They just couldn't look like you did when you came up to the counter, no kidding.

Have you been on any more trips, Harry? Guess you've been to Wales and back by now. The trip from Toronto to Ottawa would seem short to you now. There was another big raid on London this week eh? They must never feel safe over there. Have you seen an air raid shelter? They are starting the broadcasts from the Beaver Club [at Canada House in London] *again. By the way, are you still going to broadcast from Albert Hall* [in London]*? Have you played for many dances? You needed practice more on that type of music, didn't you? Duke Ellington is coming to the Aud.* [Auditorium] *next month, also Cab Calloway I understand. Don't you wish you were here? The show "Du Barry was a Lady"* [movie with Lucille Ball, Red Skelton and Gene Kelly] *with Tommy Dorsey's orchestra is on at the Capitol this week; am going to see it I think.*

I mailed a small parcel to you today; it's rather hard to make up a box when you can't bake any-thing [because she lives in a boarding house], *and it's impossible to buy candies or cookies of any kind. I will try to get my other one away to you next week. It seems so early, but you don't need to open them until Christmas!*

Wonder what you're doing tonight – maybe one of those lassies over there is taking up your time!! They tease me and tell me I can expect that. Well, maybe it's true and I'm selfish, but I'd like you to be all mine no matter how long we're separated. Do you think that's unreasonable? I may go out some, Mabel and I went to a dance last night, for a bit of diversion at the time but you are constantly with me in thought. Hope you can say the same darling. All couples seem to step out these days on each other, but I'd rather stay old-fashioned. It doesn't seem to make any difference even if they're married or not. I feel I can trust you more than anyone I've ever known anyway, darling, believe me.

You'll be getting tired reading the same old lines all the time dear, but I just start and end the day thinking about you, I can't help it. Believe me no one ever affected me like this before. Hope nothing ever happens between us. Why do I always say that? There's such an uncertainty linked with everything these days.

Wasn't that terrible about the loss of the St. Croix?[1] There'll be a good many unhappy homes, when you think of only one being saved.

I don't like saying "Goodnight" to you on paper, but I know it doesn't take as long [i.e. as it used to in person]*!! Be good to yourself; hope your cold is better and just remember, I'm always waiting for word from you and waiting for you to come back.*

With all my love, Helen

P.S. I've nearly finished my second sock, and turned the heel all by myself! Wish I could find some fine yarn to knit you a dress pair. You don't like them heavy, do you?

---

1   The HMCS St. Croix was hit and sunk by torpedoes from a German U-boat on September 20, 1943, while escorting a convoy in the North Atlantic.

4

Bournemouth

When our love was new
And each kiss an inspiration
But that was long ago
Now my consolation
Is in the stardust of a song

"Stardust," lyrics by Mitchell Parish,
music by Hoagy Carmichael

During October 1943, the RCAF band travelled by train from Wick in northern Scotland to London in the south, playing for the soldiers and civilians at military stations. On any given evening, they would play a concert, followed by a dance with either the full band or the smaller dance band. Because Harry played alto and tenor saxophone in addition to the clarinet, he often did double duty.

After a month of travelling, the band was finally back in Bournemouth. Bill, the bass player, Smitty, and Harry were warming themselves around a small fire in the grate in one of the larger rooms at the Atherstone Hotel where they were staying.

"It's good to be back home again—we've probably seen more of this island now than those who were born here," Harry said. "If I travel again when I get home, it'll have to be for a very good reason."

"Brr—I didn't realize it got so cold and damp here," Bill said. "It's only November. What's it going to be like in January?"

"I don't know, but I hope not as cold as Canada. They don't have furnaces here, just those little heaters," said Smitty, rubbing his hands together.

"We'll have to find more wood, or else come up with a load of shillings to feed those hungry heaters." Harry was always worrying about money.

"Smitty, did you wear that shirt for the whole thirty days we were gone?" Bill liked to bug him.

"Yeah, so, what's it to you? Saves on precious time, time that could be spent doing other things, like writing in a diary or reading the complete works of Shakespeare, if you've ever heard of him."

"It's bad enough when they pack eight of us into those tiny train compartments. Now that we can spread out a bit, and breathe some fresh air, I don't want to smell your fragrant aroma."

"It wouldn't be a bad idea to do some laundry before we leave for London on Saturday," Harry suggested. "I have thirty pairs of socks to wash. And Helen's knitting me another pair, but I probably won't get it till Christmas."

"How many letters did you get yesterday?" Bill was envious.

"Eighteen, plus the parcel. Oh yeah, does anyone want some Christmas cake or fudge?" Harry passed around the tin, gloating a little in his good fortune.

"Wow, those are good, considering they've been in transit for a couple of months. Does Helen have any friends who might want to write me love letters or send me food?"

"I don't know, Bill. They'd have to be pretty desperate to send you anything," Harry teased. "But I'll mention it to her in the next letter. She's pretty cheesed off at me right now. In her last letter she said she hadn't heard from me in over a week and thought I must have another girlfriend. I better keep writing as often as I can so she doesn't go off with someone else."

"Bill, why not check out the local dolls at the next dance? We've got a pretty good vantage point from the stage—we can pick and choose, so to speak," said Smitty.

"Good idea."

"Oh, here's everybody," Bob said, opening the door. "Does anyone want to hear the new V-Disc by Captain Glenn Miller?[1] I picked it up in London."

"Sure. What's on it?"

"'Stormy Weather' and 'Stardust' by the Army Air Forces Training Command Orchestra. 'St. Louis Blues' is on the flip side." Bob read the red-and-white label on the 78 rpm.

As they listened, Bill said, "Maybe we can convince Steve to let us play those songs. Harry, you could take the alto solos."

"We'd have to play them by ear. I haven't seen a new piece of sheet music since we arrived here two months ago. Well, I better go and start on a letter to Helen. She's threatened to stop writing if she doesn't hear from me soon."

---

1   The Glenn Miller Band was one of the most famous big bands entertaining troops at that time. Miller broadcast and recorded many popular songs of the day, such as "Chattanooga Choo Choo" and "In the Mood." V-Discs, short for Victory Discs, were recorded especially for the troops.

RCAF dance band playing in Loughborough, England. Harry Culley is playing tenor saxophone, third from right

Bournemouth, Oct. 25 - Nov. 4, 1943 [excerpts]

Dearest Helen,

I can't imagine why you haven't had more letters honey, unless I've been writing things I shouldn't and the censors have held them up. Anyway I hope you'll try and understand and I promise to write more often. It makes me feel pretty rotten to know that you have to wait so long.

I'm very happy to hear that you are going to Toronto at last. I think the change will do you a lot of good even though you mightn't have as many friends. Still if you have to live in a city you might just as well live in a big city. That's what I always say anyway. My mother hopes you will get some place close to her.

Of course you're just fooling when you ask me if I have another girlfriend. Still I guess it's only natural to wonder a little bit when you don't receive mail when you expect it. However you don't have to worry about me (as if you didn't already know that). I think there are enough Canadians to look after all the girls over here anyway. They seem to need it! As far as I'm concerned women don't interest me over here in the least because Smitty doesn't bother with them and there are thousands of things one can do besides dancing (which I don't care for anyway).

I've taken that rebuke about not writing to heart and will try to do better in future. I wished I could have been there to wish you many happy returns of the day darling with a big kiss [on her birthday on October 8]. *I hope you will forgive me for not remembering the exact date. I hope you like the flowers. I also forgot to sign my name on the card so I thought I'd better tell you who they're from. Don't doubt for a minute sweetheart that you are always in my thoughts.*

We went into a tea shop about 3:30 this afternoon and ordered tea. The waitress asked us whether we wanted high tea or low tea. Right away we were thrown for a loss. So we had to ask the difference and found out low tea was tea and buns and high tea was tea with chips and bacon which is the national meal over here. For variety you can get chips with sausage that never saw a pig. The Canadian Clubs in London and Bournemouth serve excellent meals for service men, especially the Legion where we stay when in London and the Salvation Army. Even very aged ladies are serving out tea cakes at their parish canteens. It's wonderful to watch them toddle around as busy as bees.

Well Darling I'll have to close for now as the boys want me to sit in on a euchre game. Goodnight sweetheart and take care of yourself until I see you again.

All my love darling Harry.

5
New Job in Toronto

For the first time, I've fallen in love
And in no time, at all
This "want you near me" feeling
Is so new to me

"For the First Time," by Dick Haymes

Helen was glad that the farewell party at the Department of Munitions and Supply was over. Lois, her co-worker, had cleared off the desks and served out the cake she had made for the occasion. Helen didn't like being the centre of attention, especially when people kept asking her uncomfortable questions, such as why she was leaving and when she had last heard from Harry.

She especially felt uneasy when her boss Mr. Lauson and Richie in shipping had insisted that she kiss them goodbye. She did it reluctantly, thinking that she wished she'd been kissing Harry instead. Helen looked down at the gold bracelet and matching brooch that were her going-away gifts from the office staff—very generous, considering she'd been there just two years.

Helen Reeder (left) and her friend and co-worker Lois Wilson

Passengers were gathering on the platform for the 3 p.m. train to Toronto. She was waiting in line for the baggage tags for her trunk and suitcases. Helen had ever so carefully wrapped the teacup and saucer from the girls at Mrs. Nesbitt's house, and now just hoped that her dishes didn't get broken along the way.

She looked up when she heard her name being called and saw Eleanor, Mabel, Lois, and Ibby running toward her.

"Thank goodness you haven't left yet," Ibby said.

"We just had to come down and see you off." Mabel was out of breath.

"We're going to miss you so." Lois hugged her and started crying. "Where are you staying tonight?"

"I've booked a room for three nights at the YWCA. I'll just take a taxi from Union Station." Helen was trying to sound confident, but it was all she could do not to cry also. She felt sick at the thought of leaving them all, unsure of what the future held.

"Just remember, Helen, if you can't find a job or a place to live, come out to Halifax with me and join the Canadian Women's Army Corps. We're leaving Ottawa next week. Everything's taken care of—your work, room, board, uniforms—plus you get paid!" Ibby had spent the better part of the last month trying to get her and Lois to enlist in the CWACs, as they were known. Helen still had the brochure in her purse. But she knew Harry's views on that subject. He didn't want her to join up. She wasn't sure why, exactly. Maybe he thought it was too dangerous or not ladylike. At any rate, she was on her way to Toronto, let the chips fall where they may.

Ottawa, Oct. 26 - Nov.5, 1943 [excerpts]

Darling Harry,

I am sitting here waiting for the transfer to come for my baggage; with rather an uncertain feeling as to what the future holds. I've had a hectic day, dashing here and there, and they had a farewell party for me at the office. They presented me with a lovely gold bracelet and brooch to match, and I was so pleased, as you know jewellery is something I very seldom buy for myself!! Can you feature me having to <u>kiss</u> some of the men goodbye? Well, I did in a very formal way, just because they considered themselves very good friends of mine!!

I received a nice cup and saucer from the girls at the [boarding] *house; something I like too. Different people have asked me why I'm moving to Toronto instead of the West* [i.e. Saskatchewan, where her parents live], *sometimes I wonder myself!! You may not hear from me as often for awhile until I get organized. Sometimes I wish I were in the service so I wouldn't have to worry*

Love in the Air

about a place to live, a place to work, etc., but I'm afraid I'd get so accustomed to it that I couldn't be independent afterwards. Ibby is leaving Rockcliffe this weekend as they've finished their course. They are having a big dinner at the Chateau [Laurier Hotel in Ottawa] *before they leave. Both she and her sister intend to go to the East Coast. She said she was sure if she could talk to Lois and me for an hour she could convince us we'd like it if we joined. We would both go against all who knew us if we did, but still there wouldn't be anything wrong with it, I guess. They hope to both get overseas eventually – her sister is engaged to a Lieutenant over there.*

[Later] *It was a lovely day for travelling, and I enjoyed my first half of the trip, then the queerest, lonesome feeling came over me, and I began to think about you and cried a little. I wanted you so much at that moment; you were a part that wasn't there and yet I had a feeling that I was doing what you wanted me to.*

So long, sweetheart. Write.

All my love, Helen

Ibby (left) and Helen, Ottawa, 1943

Bournemouth, November 16, 1943 [excerpt]

Darling Helen,

Received your air letters written 26th *and 30*[th] *also an airgraph when we came home yesterday.*

It was nice of the office staff to give you those nice things but you might have expected they'd want something in return. There's always a catch in those kinds of gifts! Oh well, I don't blame them I guess!

I suppose we'll be quite busy around Christmas time; which will be pretty lonesome. The holly bushes will be coming out in berries pretty soon I guess; but there are still lots of flowers around growing in gardens: some roses too!

Well darling I hope you are settled by now. I'll bet Mrs. Nesbitt will miss you around there.

I don't suppose this letter will excite you very much but I don't seem to have much on my mind at present as the bridge players are getting quite loud. I am looking forward to a feed of crackers and cheese some of the boys received in a package tonight.

I haven't opened your gift yet so I guess I can keep it until Christmas. I'd like to send you something nice honey but we're not allowed to send money or anything through the mail so I guess you'll have to be satisfied with flowers!

Well darling I'll close for now and run over and mail this right away as much as I hate to leave this fire. Does that prove how much I love you or doesn't it!

I wish this damn war was over!

Well good-night darling.

All my love, Harry

* * *

Rooming houses were common in Canadian cities before and during the Second World War. With so many men overseas, families often had spare bedrooms available. The rent money provided much-needed income for women, many of whom were on their own due to widowhood or husbands serving away from home. Upon her arrival in Toronto, after searching for several days, Helen found a room in a house on Winnett Avenue near Bathurst Street and St. Clair Avenue.

Helen looked around her new bed-sitting room. There was an easy chair by the window, a studio couch on the opposite wall, a small bed, a two-burner hot plate on a tin table, and a painted, chipped chest. Not as large or cozy as her room at Mrs. Nesbitt's in Ottawa, but it would have to do for now. She might as well unpack her trunk and suitcases, even though she knew she couldn't fit all of her possessions into those three small drawers and the tiny closet. Helen wondered if she would ever have a place of her own, where she didn't have to listen to strange voices downstairs, a radio blaring in the next room, or the crying of other people's children. She dared to dream about the home she and Harry might have after they got married, and how it would be with him after their time apart. But first, he would have to come home safely and come over for a cup of tea.

Ever the practical one, Helen turned her attention to finding a job in order to pay the monthly rent of $20 to Mrs. McInnis, her new landlady. She had $40 saved from her job at the Department of Munitions and Supply that would last her for a few weeks. She unfolded the flyer she'd picked up at Toronto's Union Station—it was for the Selective Service Employment Agency. She'd have to figure out how to get there.

The next morning she made her way downtown. She was surprised to see a female streetcar driver on St. Clair Avenue— women certainly could do anything they wanted to now, she thought. The driver told Helen to sit behind her so that she could let her know where to get off.

Once Helen reached the agency, she was confronted with slim pickings. Most of the jobs didn't pay the $25 a week (worth about $350 in today's currency) that she'd earned in Ottawa. She thought government jobs were probably higher paying than most. But there was one opening at the Toronto Transportation Commission (now the Toronto Transit Commission), a vacancy at the Bathurst branch for a cashier and stenographer. Helen decided to see about it.

The manager asked her to take both IQ and stenographic tests, which she did on the spot and handed in. They phoned her the next day to offer her the job. She agreed and was surprised to learn there were fifty female drivers in the motor division—that meant the establishment must have been used to having women work there. Maybe her employers wouldn't be too hard on her while she learned her new duties.

She couldn't wait to tell Harry all her good news. As she unpacked her trunk with her pen, her ink bottle, and one of the airgraph papers she'd bought at the post office before she'd left Ottawa, she found a handkerchief he'd left after one of his visits. Putting it up to her nose, she caught a whiff of his Old Spice aftershave and remembered his lingering kisses and tender caresses.

Toronto, Nov. 5 - Dec. 10 1943 [excerpts]

Darling Harry,

Believe it or not, I'm here at last and feel fairly settled after a hectic week. I haven't even had a spare minute before to write you darling, that's a fact. You will be almost a week without any mail, but hope you don't mind too much. Mine hasn't been forwarded yet either, and I've missed it terribly too. I just wrote Mrs. Nesbitt a note to give my address and have it sent down.

Monday morning I went down to Selective Service for a position, about 9:30 and there were about twenty ahead of me, imagine! They didn't give me much encouragement and said they didn't have many positions at the salary I had been getting [in Ottawa]. I got an open permit and went to see a few of Mr. Lauson's [her former boss'] friends but either the positions were taken or they were only paying $20 a week. Then I went to the

Joanne Culley

Transportation Commission, there was a vacancy at their Bathurst Branch for a cashier and stenographer with a fair salary, but it entailed a bit of night work. I came home and thought about it, then went back the next morning and wrote an IQ and stenographic test, which wasn't easy, but I must have passed, because they phoned and asked me if I wanted to start work Wednesday morning and I decided to take it. It's quite a distance from downtown, you know over on Davenport, and the offices aren't very large. The work is so different too; I was on cash all day today and found it a bit nerve-wracking. About every month or six weeks we'll be on one week nights; I hope it doesn't bother me too much. I just wonder how conditions will be here after the war when positions are so scarce now, but then I suppose there won't be so many married women working.

Guess what I have in front of me now sweetheart – your gorgeous <u>red</u> roses [which he sent for her birthday]. *Thanks so much; it was such a surprise and nothing could have pleased me more. Their perfume just fills the room. You are so thoughtful, aren't you? Apparently you wired the florist at Ottawa and someone referred them to the Y.W.* [C.A.] *because that's where I received the message asking for my address. I just cried because I was happy at the thought of what they meant, darling.*

I phoned your Mother Monday night; she wanted me to come up . . . so I went down Wednesday. Oh, darling, imagine the feeling I had going up those steps, and the memories! It was grand to see them again, and they made me feel perfectly at home (as you always said they would). Everything was *just the same as it was that last <u>Friday</u> night, and I felt so close to you when I saw all your pictures around.*

I'm in a bed sitting room; rather comfortable; I'm the only roomer. I can get my own breakfast, also my other meals but I expect I will eat dinner out. It's a long way from downtown, but fairly close to my work, so hope it will work out satisfactorily. By the way, we get a book of tickets, so have free transportation. I phoned your Mother after I decided to take it. Immediately, she asked me which number, and told me you had lived at <u>16</u> before you moved to the apartment, what a coincidence eh? [the Culley family had lived at 16 Winnett, but lost the house during the Depression.] *She told me to watch for the house that you played around for about sixteen years. I noticed it tonight; it has a red roof, with a white verandah and two big windows in front upstairs. Is that the way it used to be, or do you remember? This district has certainly been built up; your folks were saying when they built here there were only about three houses and the rest were green fields (where you used to play.)*

I don't feel so strange now that I know that! I get so sentimental, or do you think so? I can't help it when I think about you, oh, how I want you to come back soon, darling!

I unpacked my trunk tonight and found that two of my cups and one tea plate were broken to my set, which made me a bit provoked as I had six of everything, but maybe Lois can get them for me again. I have to write them all in due time. Most of them thought it was strange for me to leave all I knew there. I haven't slept much the last few nights, just the strain of everything as it isn't easy by any means, but guess everybody does it at some time or another in their life.

All my suitcases are here in the middle of the floor – haven't even hung my clothes up yet. Oh yes, I have a radio too; can only get a couple of stations but it will keep me from getting too lonely now that I haven't a room-mate. Can you get Canadian stations there? I suppose not.

I'm listening to "Waltz Time," some of the new numbers are nice. What kind of music do they go in for there at dances? Are jitterbugs ever in the spotlight? Yes, it's a bit of a change for you to play dances too, instead of parades all the time. They are singing that song "For the First Time" – do you know it?

I'll have to wander around Queen's Park one of these days and look for a particular spot [where Harry proposed to her.]

I must say "Goodnight" now sweetheart. Hope all is well with you. Your love is with me always. Be good.

Yours forever, xxx Helen

Bournemouth, Nov. 22, 1943 [excerpt]

Dear Helen,

Your airmail letters of the fifth and seventh came today and I was so glad to hear from you again although Mother was keeping me pretty well posted on how you were making out [after moving to Toronto]. *It certainly took a lot of spunk to do what you did darling and to think it was all on account of me! But then I guess there's nothing we wouldn't do for each other?*

. . . I'm sure Mother will be glad of your company any time you care to drop down but make sure there's nobody else there if all you do is talk about me. It would be pretty boring for a third person to listen to you two talk about me all night!

I opened your gift tonight [her Christmas present to him] *and I don't care if you do scold me I'm glad I did you see I knew what it was anyway and as I was packing my things into a kit bag preparing to leave tomorrow I thought I might just as well have the use of it. But I didn't expect that terrific photograph of you to be in there too.* [Helen had a glamour shot taken before she left Ottawa]. *Just think what I would have missed for a whole month if I hadn't opened it!!! You've made me happier than I ever thought possible darling and just the odd glance at it during the day will make me feel closer to you sweetheart.*

All my love, Harry

6

Leave in Oxford

There is no greater love
In all the world, it's true
No greater love
Than what I feel for you

"There Is No Greater Love," lyrics by Marty
Symes, music by Isham Jones

The band members and other service personnel received regular leave, from two days to a week or more, when they could relax in their rooms or visit nearby towns and cities. On one of their first leaves, Harry and Smitty decided to visit Oxford, about a two-hour train ride from Bournemouth. During the war, British families opened up their homes to the travelling military personnel and rented out rooms for a modest price. By 1943, British citizens were very appreciative of the Canadians, especially considering the battering that their country endured throughout the early years of the war.

Harry and Smitty were staying in different billets during their week in Oxford, but met up during the day to go sightseeing.

"So, how was your night?" Harry asked his friend.

"Wonderful—fresh sheets, sunshine streaming through the window, AND BREAKFAST IN BED!"

"No kidding—what did you do to deserve that?"

"I think Miss Fairfax has always wanted to have a man in the house, and finally her wish came true," Smitty casually replied, yawning while stretching his arms.

"You're getting too spoiled. Well, I enjoyed reading the morning paper, while sipping tea with my toast and marmalade and EGG."

"Wow, I'm impressed. Your first egg over here. I should be so lucky."

"I think we're going to be thoroughly British by the end of this war."

"Oh, I almost forgot, Miss Fairfax has invited us both to join her tonight to hear the London Symphony play at the Sheldonian Theatre."

"You don't say. You must have charmed the pants off her. Don't get any ideas."

"No fears. She must be pushing sixty. She's a piano teacher and I think she's happy to have a real live musician stay with her."

The two spent the day walking around the colleges and grounds of the historic Oxford University.

"Wouldn't you love to come back here after the war to study?" Smitty asked.

"Maybe your marks were good enough, but I was lucky to scrape by grade twelve, and that was several years ago now," Harry said.

"Let's at least go in the Bodleian just to say we've been there, in case it gets bombed, never to be seen again, like the cathedral in Coventry."

"Perish that thought."

As they entered the historic library and gazed at the stacks rising to the ceiling, Harry thought about how tragic it would be to lose all of those ancient tomes. There was so much history in England—and all over Europe, for that matter. He hoped the war would be over before there was much more destruction. How he wished that Helen could share in all that he was experiencing. But for now, he'd have to settle for the next best thing, which was to write to her about it in a letter.

Bournemouth, Nov. 26, Dec. 2, 1943 [excerpts]

Darling Helen,

Well, we're back in the traces again after a very charming visit to Oxford.

I stayed at the home of a war worker and daughter. It was a very nice home and naturally I had my own room. Her son is away at Cambridge. I got up in the morning when I felt like it (I'm always up before Al [Smitty] *incidentally), then we went out sightseeing for the day.*

They kept three ducks in the back yard and I had my first duck egg yesterday and also my first egg over here. I'd almost forgotten what they tasted like, no kidding.

Would you ask Mother how to make egg toast [French toast] *as the lady in Oxford asked me to send the recipe.*

I'm glad to be back though [in Bournemouth], *to get down to work again.*

Things aren't as comfortable as when Lewis had this place [the former owner of the Atherstone Hotel] *as the new guy is very short of cupboards and drawers and also the beds are pretty bumpy, but I suppose we'll give him a chance anyway.*

Well dearest I'm glad to hear you are getting along so well, I know I have nothing to worry about in regards to you and I'm living up to my end of the bargain too.

Will close for now honey. I love you as I always will.

Harry

RCAF bandmates on leave, Harry Culley on right

Toronto, December 12 and 14, 1943[excerpts]

Dearest Harry,

Just finished reading your letters over again and thanks for the card which you sent of Christchurch. It was handed to me last night, along with your three pictures; your Mother got them yesterday morning. We think you are looking very well darling, much better than you did in Ottawa. It must have been your night life down here I guess!!

I like the one outside your house [at the Atherstone], *you look so gay and young – maybe it's because you haven't a moustache! You'll grow it again though won't you? It was foolish of me to think you would change in four months, but then I'm always getting ideas like that.*

We didn't expect our parcels would arrive so soon but that's better than being too late I guess. Seeing that you enjoy crackers so well, I'll have to send some the next time, I was told they didn't pack well and they took up so much room in the box so I didn't bother putting them in. Your Mother does a good deal of baking on her rations, and every-thing is always good too! I guess Ross [Harry's younger brother] *always knows where to find the cake tin when he comes home. Did that used to be a habit of yours? It isn't hard to get Christmas cakes here* [in Toronto] *but at the time I sent your parcel, that was the only one I could find after walking up Bank and Elgin Streets* [in Ottawa]. *They never taste as nice as the home-baked ones though. I sent Mother some raisins and currants, because they can't get them there. There are more canned vegetables in the stores now too.*

Oh yes, I told your Mother about that recipe for egg toast and she's going to look it up for you. She laughed as it reminded her of the time you sent the shortbread recipe home. She's going to show me the letter.

Yes, darling, I know in my heart that someday you will prove what you told me, and you say you are living up to it now, how perfect it is to hear that! I'll do my best too, but it isn't easy, and it never will be forced. It's the will and the dreams behind it that make things work out successfully, don't you think so? We want our love to be strong enough that we'll do anything for each other.

It's time to leave you again darling. You know I don't like saying good night any time, not even on paper. Won't it be swell if someday we won't have to? Hope everything is first rate with you, and my love is with you always.

xxx Helen.

7
Christmas 1943

Dancing with my darling
Here the shadow lies
I can still remember the thrill
When I have kissed you goodnight

"Dancing with My Darling," lyrics by Mitchell
Parish, music by Jean Delettre

It was the first time Helen had ever worked on Christmas Day. She was glad her mother didn't know. The most she had let them do on the farm was to milk the cows or feed the chickens—and cook dinner, of course. Other than that, it was a day of rest.

However, there was a war on and Helen had a job where the buses and streetcars had to run every day, holiday or not, so she just had to accept it. Plus, it was better to be working than sitting at home missing Harry.

It had been a busy day, just her and her friend and co-worker Kay on cashier duty to count the money the drivers brought in after their shifts.

After punching out at five o'clock, she made her way over to Harry's parents' brownstone apartment on Isabella Street in downtown Toronto.

"Merry Christmas, Helen, would you like to have a little gin, my dear?" Harry Sr. greeted her with a kiss.

"Sure, if you're having some." Helen made her way through the hall into the living room.

"Helen, this is my mother, Mary Fernley," Ida said, getting up from the sofa to give her a hug.

"Nice to meet you."

"I'll bet you're missing Harry, especially today," said the kindly looking older woman.

"Yes, I sure wish he was here with us tonight."

"Can you turn down the volume, Ross? I know you like Bing Crosby, but we're trying to have a conversation over here," Harry Sr. admonished his younger son.

"Supper's just about ready, Helen. You can sit there, in Harry's old chair," said Ida. "Little did I dream last year that there'd be a girl at his place." She paused for a moment, smiling warmly at Helen before turning to her husband. "Harry, can you please carve the bird?"

"Let's pull the crackers," Ross said, sitting down, and at that, everyone got busy, donning their colourful paper hats and reading their fortunes.

"What does yours say, Helen?" asked Elaine, Ross's girlfriend.

"'Hope' … I hope that Harry and I can be together next year!"

"Mine's 'success'—I that means I'll make lots of money!" said Ross.

Then they all fell silent as they tucked into goose with all the trimmings, plum pudding, shortbread, and fruitcake.

"Ross, can you please pass the shortbread around? I've noticed you're keeping it pretty close to you there, but I'm sure Helen and Elaine would like to have a taste," Harry Sr. teased.

"All right, but no more than one each!" Ross reluctantly handed over the plate.

After supper, Harry Sr. and Ross, who played trombone in a dance band, as well as in the navy band, rushed off to work, as they had engagements at the Royal York Hotel and the Savarin Club, playing for the late diners. Ida, Elaine, and Helen started in on the dishes.

When Elaine went home, Ida and Helen left to make the rounds visiting other Culley relatives by streetcar.

Toronto, Dec. 23 and 26, 1943 [excerpts]

Darling Harry,

Well here it is the day after Christmas and I'm feeling like my usual self, believe it or not! Can you say the same, I wonder??? Did you enjoy yourself? Were you playing Christmas Eve and also through the day? I didn't like the idea of working yesterday either, and we were really busy as there were only two of us there. I left promptly at five, and supper was nearly ready when I arrived.

Everything was so nicely decorated, I took a couple of snaps of the tree, also one of Elaine and Ross in front of it, but suppose they won't turn out just because I want them to.

[After supper] *we called at Geneva's and Ed's* [Harry's aunt and uncle] *for a few minutes. Their little girl is sick; she said they didn't have a very nice Christmas. Geneva asked about you and wanted to see my ring. They thought I looked like Betty too* [Harry's cousin].

From there we went to Grace and Art's [Harry's aunt and uncle] *and his brother and wife, also your other grandmother and grandfather* [Kate and Teck Culley] *were there, all having a good time. Grace said she was so surprised when you received her parcel in a little over a week, and mentioned the letter and Christmas greeting they got from you. I expected your grandfather to be a bigger man, but I could see he was quite lively all right!!*

We left around 11:30 p.m., and your Mother said the party was just beginning then.

Oh yes, she gave Elaine and I each a nice set of pictures – English rose-covered cottages. I'd rather have something I could keep; she said she thought I'd be trunking [i.e. collecting items for her hope chest.] *It so happened that Elaine gave her a slip too, but she's going to change it as mine fit her better. . . I appreciated my flowers* [that Harry sent] *most though; they still look very fresh! I have them in a vase on the radio and they seem to say something every time I look at them. The best Christmas greeting would be from you in person honey, but I have to take the second best; and thanks very much for them. I'm listening to Manhattan Merry-go-Round* [on the radio] *and Thomas L. Thomas is singing "Dancing with My Darling," have you heard it? Ross has three new Bing Crosby records.*

Did you all get together and have a party as you planned? Have you any cake or treats left? It would have seemed more like Christmas to you if you hadn't received your parcels so soon. You know how they urge us to mail early over here.

Darling why do I tell you all these little things that are probably very uninteresting to you? You are a part of me, that's why and I want you so much, it hurts sometimes.

So long sweetheart; I hope I hear from you this week, and I always pray for you.

My best love, Helen xxx

Helen with flowers that Harry sent

Bournemouth, Dec. 27, 1943 and Jan. 6, 1944 [excerpts]

My Darling Helen,

Just finished reading your three letters dated 19, 23, 26 for the twentieth time at least because they reflected just how I was feeling towards you. Christmas isn't the same when you are not with the one you love. We found that out didn't we? Well anyway, you weren't alone in your loneliness like

I was. Was my grandfather dancing around like a grizzly bear and did he kiss you? He gets quite frolicsome at times; you have to watch him.

I got two more Christmas parcels – 2 lbs. of candy from my aunt and a box from my school which was a surprise. In it was a very large pair of blue woollen gloves and candy and stuff. How did you make out for Christmas? We had a terrible Christmas Eve [i.e. with the bombings] *but we got over that all right. We travelled all night from Redhill* [a town south of London] *just to get away from it; we arrived in Bournemouth about 7:30 and we were playing for the airmen's Christmas dinner at 11:30 so you see we didn't get much sleep. We rested up on Sunday so we had a big party. Boy! What a party - 70 bottles of beer and several bottles of gin and lime for 14 of us. Needless to say I didn't get too drunk. Even the S. A.* [Salvation Army] *boys were busy a week ago buying liquor for the bunch of us.*

We took some pictures so if they turn out all right I'll send them over.

I haven't had very much to tell you this time dearest as the dance band has been working very hard while the other guys laid around Bournemouth but we do have a good time amongst ourselves so that's the main thing I guess.

I managed to get a slice of turkey on Christmas. I thought you might like to know. I've got so much fruit cake it will last me all year I'll bet. I'm waiting to hear how you made out.

Joanne Culley

I hope it's the last Christmas I'll have to spend away from you dear. I guess it was very quiet for you.

Well, I'll try and make up for it when I come home. Well Darling, I really must close now as we have to get ready for the dance and will write again when I hear from you.

All my love, Harry

RCAF bandmates' Christmas celebration, Harry Culley (second row, right), Al Smith (back row, third from left)

8
Celebrity Concerts

I'll be loving you always
With a love that's true always
When the things you've planned
Need a helping hand
I will understand always

"Always," by Irving Berlin

The Royal Canadian Air Force sent five concert bands and a dance band overseas during the Second World War that played close to 3,000 performances, including concert repertoire, parade music, popular songs, and jazz.

Many of the concerts the approximately thirty-member ensemble of the RCAF No. 3 Personnel Reception Centre Band presented were for functions such as ceremonies at Canada House, the opening of a hospital wing, outdoor sports days on military bases, variety shows, performances for troops arriving and going home on ships, and more. Music by the band was also recorded by the BBC in London for broadcast to the Allied troops in Europe.

They marched in parades for military occasions, church festivities, and Victory Loan drives, bringing entertainment to the citizens in the towns and cities they visited, including performing in several official parades in London along the Mall past Buckingham Palace.

A twelve-member dance band was created from members of the larger band, with trombones, saxophones, trumpets, a bass player, and a pianist. They played dances for the army and air force officers, for troops on the bases and at the legions, at special events such as holiday parties, and as backup for travelling entertainers. The popular songs of the day they played included "Chattanooga Choo Choo," "Long Ago and Far Away," "In the Mood," "We'll Meet Again," "Starlight Serenade," and "Stardust."

Celebrity entertainers such as Jack Benny, Gracie Fields, Bob Hope, and a host of other stars visited military bases during the Second World War to provide entertainment that would lift spirits and offer a diversion from the war. Popular composer, songwriter, and musician Irving Berlin came to Bournemouth in January 1944 to give a concert for the air force personnel stationed there.

* * *

The Pavilion Theatre in Bournemouth was a five-minute walk from the Atherstone Hotel where Harry and several of the other band members boarded. Built in the 1920s, the beautiful Art Deco–style concert hall became a haven during the war years, offering entertainment for the military personnel stationed nearby. It was easily the most impressive building in town, a beacon near the English Channel. So far it had survived being bombed; in November 1943, an aerial assault had come close to the beach and pier when twenty-five bombs had been dropped and one person killed.

The band members wended their way along the hedge-lined roads to the rock garden below the Pavilion. The weather was fine, so the walk wasn't too onerous, even though they were lugging their instruments. Waves lapped onto the shore in the distance.

"Can you believe this weather? Back home there'd be piles of snow and ice everywhere," said Harry.

"Yeah, look at those palm trees—it's never really winter here, I guess," Smitty observed.

Harry adjusted his grip on his instrument case and smiled. "I'm looking forward to playing with Irving Berlin tonight at the Grand Anglo-American Ball."

"Yes, it'll be good to play some decent music—not like that old-time dance we played last week."

"That really was something. All those old ladies dancing quadrilles and lancers in their silver-and-gold slippers—English country dances from the nineteenth century." Harry let out a soft chuckle.

"Well, I'm sure it'll be quite different tonight. Berlin is one of the most popular songwriters of this century—'Blue Skies,' 'White Christmas,' 'Always'—and we're going to accompany him!" Smitty was beaming.

"Yes, I can't wait to tell Helen about it."

The band opened with the "Star-Spangled Banner," as a nod to Berlin's home country, then launched into "O Canada" and "God Save the King." They soon caught a glimpse of Berlin backstage, getting ready for the cabaret.

"My, his hair is awfully black. I bet he dyes it—he must be over fifty," Harry whispered to Ossie, who was sitting next to him on stage.

"Here he comes now," Ossie said.

The emcee announced the arrival of "America's Ambassador of Goodwill" as the band broke into "Oh! How I Hate to Get Up in the Morning," as part of his medley of military tunes.

Berlin walked on stage to applause, singing,

"I've been a soldier quite a while

Love in the Air

And I would like to state,
The life is simply wonderful,
The army food is great.
I sleep with ninety-seven others in a wooden hut.
I love them all,
They all love me,
It's very lovely but …"

After this first verse, the "Full Beauty Chorus" marched out singing from both wings of the stage and lined up in front of the band, with Berlin in the middle.

"Oh! How I hate to get up in the morning.
Oh! How I'd love to remain in bed.
For the hardest blow of all
Is to hear the bugler call,
Ya gotta get up,
Ya gotta get up,
Ya gotta get up this morning."

My sentiments exactly, thought Harry. Nothing seemed to have changed much about army life since the First World War when Berlin wrote his song. But at least Harry and his band-mates were out of the barracks for the time being.

"Good thing he's got their backup voices," said Harry at the end. "I think he's a better composer than a singer; his voice is so high."

Ossie nodded, all the while keeping his eyes on the backs of the beauties in front of them. The band accompanied the next few song-and-dance numbers, finishing up with the "High Step Sisters," then they all rushed backstage to get Berlin's signature on their programmes.

Bournemouth, Jan. 6, 1944 [excerpt]

Dearest Helen,

*Well darling, here's another day over. The band
went over very well tonight. We played for Irving
Berlin while he sang some of his old tunes . . . .*

*That's Irving Berlin's autograph on the back of the
programme. Here's a snap for you taken in the
park in Bournemouth. It's really a beautiful place
with a built-up rock garden behind us. There's
also a pool full of goldfish close by. We go through
this park on the way to rehearsals and one of
the boys stopped us to take it. Smitty is always
kidding – just like Ross.*

All my love, Harry

Toronto, Feb. 10, 1944 [excerpt]

My Darling Harry,

*Well, honey, your pictures came today, and I
think it's just swell of you all. You look very
serious but handsome! I notice you are growing a
moustache again. As a group you look well taken
care of anyway. I don't believe you've gained
much weight. I can remember seeing Smitty* [in
Ottawa] *and the one next to him, Les Allison, is
it? The girls wouldn't believe that Smitty was
only twenty-one. . . That park looks beautiful, it
reminds me of Victoria when I see the rock garden.
. . The grass stays green all winter, doesn't it? It
wouldn't have been very cold as you haven't gloves
on. Berlin's autograph is a scrawl all right. That
must have been a nice show.*

All my love, Helen

Love in the Air

RCAF band members in the lower gardens of the
Pavilion, left to right, Les Mann, Harry Culley, Ed
Evans, Ernie Shedden, Les Allison, and Al Smith

* * *

When they reached Waterloo Station in London after the two-hour trip from Bournemouth, the band members filed off the train, grabbed their instruments from the huge pile on the platform, then made their way outside to the waiting transport truck. They were whisked away on a ten-minute drive to Canada House at Trafalgar Square, where they were scheduled to play. It was the fourth anniversary of the Beaver Club, the gathering place for Canadian service personnel in the city. There was great cause for celebration, as the building had remained standing during the Blitz in 1940, even though it was nearly destroyed when a bomb had landed very close.

Paper streamers festooned the ornate, high-ceilinged hall and hand-lettered "Happy 4th Anniversary" banners hung from the walls. But the centrepiece was the huge cake in the middle of the room. The place was packed with well-wishers, both civilian and military. Excitement was in the air as word spread that the king, the queen, and other dignitaries had arrived and were at that very moment touring the building.

After tuning up, the band started in on its usual program. Harry was quite nervous and was hoping that his clarinet wouldn't squeak, that his reed wouldn't break, and that he wouldn't play a wrong note. When Steve, the bandmaster, caught a glimpse of the royal entourage out of the corner of his eye, he nodded to the band, whereupon it broke into "God Save the King." The audience rose to attention for the grand entrance. On the final note, the royal couple came over to Steve and shook his hand. Harry couldn't hear what she said to him, but Queen Elizabeth seemed to be doing all the talking. She looked quite relaxed, whereas King George's face betrayed the worries of the war.

"This is the first time I've seen Their Majesties in person," Harry whispered to Ossie. "They've been through a lot—especially during the Blitz when a bomb just barely missed their drawing room at Buckingham Palace."

"Can you hear what the queen is saying to Steve?"

"No, but look, now the king is shaking his hand, and the photographer's getting a picture of them!"

"I'll bet Gilchrist[1] will be green with envy! He's jealous enough of Steve as it is—this'll get him even more fired up."

Then it was time to cut the cake. Alice Massey, the wife of Vincent Massey, Canada's High Commissioner to Great Britain, stepped forward and served pieces to the band members first, which made them feel very honoured.

After tea and about a dozen doughnuts each, the specialty of the house, the band members had a few hours off until they had to get back to play for the dance at 7:30 p.m. Harry decided to spend his time in the theatre across the square to take in the latest Canadian army newsreels. Then he fought his way through the noisy streets to drop his bag off at the YMCA where they were staying for the night.

---

1   Another RCAF bandmaster

Alice Massey serving cake to RCAF band members, Ossie on right

After the dance, he and Smitty retreated to their room. That's when they heard a deafening noise. Harry peered through the edge of the blackout curtain to see the sky lit up with phosphorous bombs.

"It looks like they're dropping over by Whitehall, where the War Office is," Harry said. "Just our luck—the Luftwaffe are back at it now that we're in town."

"Maybe we should spend the night in the underground; we might be lucky enough to get a bunk." Smitty was worried.

"I don't know. I think I'd rather stay here, where at least there aren't any rats," Harry said.

The bombings continued throughout the night, and in the morning, both of them were weary. On their way over to Birdcage Walk for their parade past Buckingham Palace, they looked at the headlines: "The Little Blitz brings heaviest night raid on London since 1941."

"'The fortress outside the War Office was hit, as was the Horse Guards Parade near Whitehall, and the windows were blown out at No. 10 Downing Street,'" Smitty read. "'. . .

Churchill's assistant private secretary, Sir John Colville, called it a "short, sharp blitz.""

"Thank God we're leaving for York later today—hopefully it will be a little quieter there," Harry said. "Helen will kill me if I don't make it home alive!" They both laughed at that one.

Sign on London street

London, Feb. 17, Glasgow, Feb. 23, 1944 [excerpts]

Dearest Helen,

Well, this has been somewhat of a red letter day for all of us here. We had the honour to play for the King and Queen to-day! Yes, I'm not kidding. The photographer took a picture of Mrs. Vincent Massey serving the cake to the guy next to me. Dammit why couldn't it have been me? The picture is supposed to come out next Friday in the Canada Weekly paper for the Forces, so I'll send it to you sweetheart whether I'm in it or not.

We were in London last Friday night during the "little blitz" they called it. To say the least it was a little difficult sleeping through that one!

Eight of us are going up near York tomorrow to play a dance and I imagine it will be a lot colder up there.

I wonder how many more thousands of miles we'll have to travel before this is over?

Love, Harry

Toronto, Feb. 29, 1944 [excerpt]

Harry Darling,

Honey, it made me excited just reading your letter of the 17th *yesterday, telling me all about your big day. I bet you did a good deal of rehearsing for that. Were you nervous when you were playing? I don't believe I could have held the instrument! . . . Have you seen the latest postcard of them* [the Royal couple] *at home with the two Princesses? It was in the Telegram the other day.*

It would be a big event for the Beaver Club all right, and for the Canadians. .

Well, it's twilight now – it doesn't get dark until after 7:30 p.m. these nights.

My best love, Helen

9

Passing the Time at Home

This will be my shining hour
Calm and happy and bright
And in my dreams, your face will flower
Through the darkness of the night

"My Shining Hour," by Harold Arlen

Helen had just nicely returned home from work and finished making baked beans and toast on her two-burner hot plate and toaster, when she heard the doorbell ring.

Her landlady Mrs. McInnis told Ida Culley to go upstairs.

"I'm so glad you were able to come," said Helen as she invited Harry's mother in.

"Well, I have the night off, and I do need your help to figure out this double heel I'm working on for Harry's socks," Ida said, out of breath and looking around. "This is a very nice room, and it looks out onto the street."

"Yes, I'm feeling quite at home here now."

"Oh, and before I forget, here are the two letters that came today from our favourite guy."

Helen took them excitedly and read them right away. She hadn't received a letter from Harry for a couple of days.

"Sometimes yours come quickly, and ours take longer, and vice versa," Ida said, sitting down. "It's always good to know he's all right."

When she'd finished, Helen handed them back to Ida.

"Well, it sounds like they had a nice leave in Evesham. The trains always seem so crowded wherever they go," Helen said.

"I heard there was more bombing in London. . . . I hope they're not there when it's going on," Ida commented.

Helen let out a deep sigh. "Me too. I worry that at some point he's going to be in the wrong place at the wrong time. All I can do is pray for his safety."

"Best that we keep busy and not worry too much."

At that, Helen got out her knitting book and looked up the instructions for the heel.

"Let me see where you're at with it," Helen said as she studied Ida's work, and then compared it to her pattern. "Here's what you do next," she remarked, pointing to the page in her manual.

"I'll copy out the instructions just to be on the safe side," Ida said.

Helen grabbed a box that was sitting on top of her easy chair; she had started on a project folding and waxing a dozen red-and-white crepe paper roses to give to her friends.

"I think I'll send a few to my sister-in-law Beryl, as her birthday is coming up," Helen commented.

"I wouldn't mind one or two also, they're very pretty," said Ida, admiring Helen's delicate work.

"Sure."

At 7 p.m., Helen turned on the radio.

"I think Fred Waring and the Pennsylvanians are on tonight from New York. You know that Harry's uncles play in that band—George plays trumpet and Fred plays violin?" Ida asked.

Joanne Culley

"Yes, he did mention that. There's so much music in your family," Helen said.

Time flew by as they listened to the music and did their handiwork, then Helen boiled the water for tea.

It was late. "Well, I should be going; we're rehearsing all day tomorrow and I don't want to be too tired," Ida said. "Thanks for a nice evening, Helen."

Toronto, Jan. 21 – Feb. 5, 1944 [excerpts]

Darling Harry,

Last night I was through work at 4:30 and just sitting there wondering what I was going to do for the night when your Mother called and asked if it would be all right if she came up to see me. I was so pleased, as I had asked her different times, but it's quite a distance for her to come . . . We had a cup of tea around eleven – if you could have only dropped in about that time! I walked up to the streetcar with her; and she was telling me who lived where, etc. She said it was the first time she'd been by the house since you left.

Honestly darling when I talk to her about you, one who knows you so well, I almost feel as though I've seen you.

There doesn't seem to be much on the radio now. Last night we enjoyed it though – Waltz Time, a symphony, Fred Waring, etc. Thursday is a good night too. Mart Kenny is playing out at the [Palace] Pier tonight, but you can't surprise me at the last minute and say we're going this time or do you remember that?

Have you heard that song "My Shining Hour?" Frank Sinatra sang it last night and Bing Crosby sang "My Ideal".

You have likely heard that Lt. Gen. McNaughton is back in Canada and holidaying at the Seigniory Club in Quebec. We hear there's quite a bit of action in London these nights. Naturally, we think things too, but keep praying for you and all the others.

Well, I suppose I should go and catch forty winks, but I don't feel tired. It's getting windy out and looks like rain. Thank goodness it isn't cold.

I have a letter box up on the wall with _every_ one of your letters in. Your Mother thought I'd have to put some of them away soon.

Must go now, should be getting more mail one of these days.

Bye dear. Always yours,

With love, Helen

* * *

Helen wasn't supposed to work the evening shift at the TTC that night, but her co-worker Ruth's husband was in town on a weekend leave from Sault Ste. Marie, and Helen knew that if she were in that position, she would want someone to fill in for her.

When she arrived at the office, Edith commented on how nice her hair looked.

"I'm trying a different style, wearing it loose instead of up." Helen was a little embarrassed. "I'm not sure if Harry will like it or not, but I'm sending him a photo to get his opinion. He does seem interested in all these little details."

"You sure do miss him, don't you?" Edith said.

"Yes. I'd give anything to see him once a month. Ruth doesn't know how lucky she is."

Helen got to work adding up the minutes and hours from the drivers' schedules and trying to make them balance. Standing for a long time on the cement floor at the wicket was hard on her feet. She had asked her boss Mr. Brown to get the cashiers some high stools, but so far, none had materialized. At least she had to do it only one week a month—the rest of the time she spent doing stenography, typing, and answering phones.

The drivers came in late that evening. They'd been delayed because of the major snowstorm and a parade up Yonge Street launching the next big drive for the Red Cross.

"We were held up at least twenty minutes, so everyone is off their schedules," Barry moaned. "Don't tell the boss."

"Don't worry, he went home at 4:30 p.m., so he doesn't need to know," said Helen. She didn't get along with Mr. Brown as well as she had with Mr. Lauson in Steel Control. However, she did try to keep on his good side, such as when she went out to get his lunch the week before, riding on the St. Clair streetcar with the inspector. Now and then she saw his sense of humour, but as a rule, she thought he was very reserved.

They worked steadily until 8 p.m., when the hubbub finally died down. She took her supper break and spent the time trying to figure out her finances. She'd just received a windfall in the mail the day before—$85 from the retirement fund from the Department of Munitions and Supply in Ottawa. But new this year, she'd have to pay 5 percent income tax on her salary of $1,250 a year (or $24 a week).[1] *It comes in one door and goes out the other*, she thought. She wanted to make sure she

---

1   The average annual salary at that time was about $2,400, and women made about half of that.

was putting enough away in her savings account for when she and Harry started their lives together.

Toronto, Feb. 23, 1944

Dearest Harry,

On Monday I received your letter of the 2nd and 3rd - you tell me much more than you did at first and are becoming a good correspondent, no kidding! You did say once that you couldn't write letters; it must be the practice you're getting.

This week I'm on the evening shift, 4:30 p.m. to 12:30 a.m., so this is being written in the early morning hours. I can write better at night than in the daytime. It has been snowing; the trees are all capped in white and it's a beautiful night. It seems funny for me to be around in the daytime, but I seem to always find something to keep me busy. I want to go downtown, maybe Friday and your Mother may come with me, as I have to shop around for a coat again. The only thing is on this shift, one has no night life; if you were here that would really go hard on me. Yet the other girls don't mind in the least.

We have the radio on part of the time while at work, and I try to listen to it when I'm doing about sixty words a minute. Gee! I don't know if I can even go that fast now or not. Anyway, we heard Guy Lombardo and Tommy Dorsey. It's only a small radio but we can get all the stations. By the way, they played that piece I can't forget – I bet you don't know what it is [perhaps "Always" by Irving Berlin].

I told you about getting $85 back from my retirement fund, didn't I? I'm banking what I can as I make it too honey, just like you are. There's no reason why we can't start in where we left off is there?? I'm just wondering, like everybody else just how much my last 5% of income tax will be. It has to be in by April but the forms aren't out yet. The deduction is $10 more on my salary here than in Ottawa. I must say you are well paid for travelling around; more than you expected, isn't it? Then too, as you say, the experience really means something to you.

Darling, I don't see how you can ever find time to think about me or yourself, unless it's when you're on the train. I keep repeating the last three lines of this letter over and over and over again, and praying that we'll always be the same.

Bye now honey. My love always.

Helen. xxx

TTC co-workers (l to r) Helen Reeder, Kathleen (Kay) Mackay and Edith Fader

Love in the Air

* * *

It didn't take Helen long to create a supportive social network around her, even though she'd been in Toronto for just three months. She made friends easily, and she re-connected with relatives in order to help her get through the time while Harry was overseas.

She was lucky that her four cousins, the daughters of her father's brother Art Reeder, had all come from Saskatchewan to work in Toronto. Billie (Arabelle), Georgie (Georgina), Glady (Gladys), and Donny (Donna) were from Craik, Saskatchewan, about 150 miles south of Thaxted, where Helen's family lived. The sisters all worked at the John Inglis Company that manufactured small arms: Billie as an inspector, Georgie in the lab, and the other two on the manufacturing line. The factory made weapons such as Bren machine guns, autocannons, and pistols for the Allies. After the war, it switched to making appliances.

Helen and Georgie, who was about her age, became good friends and spent a lot of time together.

"What a lovely apartment you have here," Helen said as she took off her coat and entered her cousins' flat.

"Yes, we were lucky to find it: two bedrooms, a kitchen, and a living room," said Georgie. "We have to eat in the kitchen, but that's all right, as we're not always here at once, with everyone on shifts. Billie and I share a bedroom, and Glady and Donny share the other. It's good that we can split the rent four ways." She then added, "We're so glad you're in Toronto now too. Funny how so many Saskatchewan girls have come east."

"Well, I guess it's because of all the work here," said Helen.

"Ted is the only one at home now, helping Dad on the farm," Glady remarked.

"He's the youngest, right?" asked Helen.

"Yes, our father was so happy when Ted came along, after five girls. That's why three of us have boys' nicknames. His wish finally came true," Billie chimed in.

"Have you heard from Harry lately?" Georgie asked.

"Yes, I got a couple of letters this week. They seem to take about two weeks now, so I'm happy. Oh, and he sent me a photo of the dance band in the lower gardens at Bournemouth—here, I brought it with me. Harry's on the right, and that's his good friend Smitty."

"Oh, Smitty's cute—maybe I could date him when he comes home," said Donny, leaning over to look at the photo.

"He's only twenty-one, so just a little older than you are," Helen replied.

"Well, let's eat. Helen and I are going to the art gallery after supper, and it's open only until 9 p.m.," said Georgie.

Toronto, Jan. 12 - June 11, 1944 [excerpts]

Dearest Harry,

You have certainly been good to me the last few days; yesterday I got your letter of the 6th [of January] *and today your postcards were waiting for me. That letter was a month coming by air mail; it must have been waylaid somewhere. I found it so interesting, and I like to feel that I know a bit about what you're doing and seeing. . .*

Tonight I went from work to my cousins for supper – they work in Small Arms; one in the lab and the other as Inspector. We talked, looked at pictures, ate, then Georgie and I went to the Art Gallery, where they had this exhibition of fine art; proceeds in aid of the Merchant Marine. There were some marvellous paintings; one could just stand and look at some of them for hours. We both enjoyed it thoroughly. There was a large crowd of people there. They showed the equipment of a seaman when at sea, with lifebelt, waterproof equipment, emergency rations, etc. They have a light on their skull cap which flashes on and off in order to attract attention. Afterwards we went for lunch at a little place near the Ford Hotel then I caught the Bay streetcar. It's snowing again very softly and it's very mild. This will probably all melt now. Georgie and I are great company for each other, and I'm glad, but I wish they lived closer by.

My youngest cousin (she's about seventeen) [Donny] *was telling me about her date with a First Lieutenant to go to the Royal York last night. She was so excited. The last time I saw her, she just couldn't stand the sight of boys.*

Darling, it makes me so happy to know that after you've been around so much you can sit down, read my letters and remember the little things we've done. Yes, I've thought about that day too [i.e. when they went walking in the Gatineau Hills]. *We were really alone out there but not for long. We walked so far, and talked about a lot of things. We could do that now; well, even thinking about it brings a strong feeling back again. We didn't succeed in that regard here, only about a half hour before train time, and how quickly it passed! The future must bring us together always just as you say. There will likely be things to stand in our way but we will have to overcome them.*

We had a very busy day, and my feet are tired from walking after standing all day. Otherwise I'm feeling all right, and have escaped the cold, which everyone else seems to have. My cousin has a terrible one, but that night work just about gets her down as she has two weeks at a time, but they won't after this month. The four of them are so happy-go-lucky, and think I should be more that way. You agree with them I guess don't you? I could never take anything lightly somehow. They have lots of boyfriends and go out a lot.

Friday night Kay [from work], *Georgie and I went to the Navy program. It was very fine and lots of variety. Ross* [Harry's brother who plays trombone in the Navy band] *was in the second row; we finally caught a glimpse of him and he recognized me. Their Glee Club sang a few numbers before intermission. They played "Springtime" which I like, a cornet trio and the last number was "Musical Switch". They had a Sports Programme which was very comical. Your Grandmother was there but I didn't see her; there was a large crowd. It was over around 10:15 and Ross went to the Queensway after that. We came back to the Varsity on Bloor and had lunch, then from there I went to work.*

No, I don't exactly worry when you don't write, as I keep thinking there's one on the way, and I try not to imagine things. I just have to retire now honey, before I go to sleep in this chair. This week has certainly gone by quickly. I _must_ *be at home on Sunday night at 8:30 to listen to the broadcast* [i.e. of Harry's parents' duo piano show].

Well, sweetheart how quickly the minutes fly when I'm occupied with thoughts of you! I shall be waiting, always waiting – you can depend on that.

My best love, Helen.

Bournemouth, June 30, 1944 [excerpt]

Dear Helen,

I picked out several pictures of the dance band taken on the "Canada Day" Tour and will send you some when I get them.

The fellow who sleeps next to me [Bill] *seemed quite interested in Georgie* [Helen's cousin]. *He's very good looking, dark, and single. He plays bass.*

All my love, Harry

Toronto, Aug. 2, 1944 [excerpt]

My Darling Harry,

I was talking to Georgie awhile ago and mentioned that I was giving Bill her address. Our surnames are the same [i.e. Reeder] *Her address is 17 Lansdowne Avenue. Telephone La. 8233- how's that? She's very anxious to hear from him . . .*

Love and kisses, Helen

10
D-Day and After

Chills run up and down my spine
Aladdin's lamp is mine
The dream I dreamed was not denied me
Just one look and then I knew
That all I longed for long ago was you

"Long Ago and Far Away," lyrics by Ira
Gershwin, music by Jerome Kern

During the spring of 1944, the band travelled around the
Midlands by train playing Victory Loan dances, its members
living like transients out of their kit bags. Harry wondered if his
three shirts could last a month, and they did—he thought Helen
would be proud of how he could wash and iron his uniform, no
matter how difficult the conditions.

After living in the barracks on fifteen different military stations, they were glad to be back at the Atherstone Hotel in
Bournemouth, especially now that spring had arrived.

"I think this is the most beautiful spot in England, it's so
fragrant with the tulip and cherry trees in blossom," Harry

said to Smitty on their way over to rehearsal through the lower gardens.

"Is that a cuckoo that's been singing like mad all the way along?"

"Yep, sounds just like the clock."

Looking over the calm waters of the English Channel, they could see that the beach was still cordoned off with barbed wire and the middle section of the famous Bournemouth pier was missing.

Bournemouth pier through barbed wire

Al Smith (left) and Harry Culley on
Bournemouth beach with barbed wire

Joanne Culley

"Do you think the pier was bombed earlier in the war?" Harry asked.

"No, I heard that the citizens removed sixty feet of it themselves so that no invaders could use it as a landing," Smitty said.

The stage at the Pavilion Theatre looked the same, and most of the band members were already there, setting up.

"If we have to play 'Take the "A" Train' one more time, I think I'll be sick," Ossie grumbled as he put his clarinet together.

"I wish they'd send more music over for us. Don't they realize we need a change now and then?" Harry said.

After the rehearsal, Steve tapped the music stand.

"I know we're all exhausted from that last tour, and you guys did a wonderful job—the officers at Warrington said you sounded great—but I've just received word that we have to clear out again."

At that announcement, there was a collective groan.

"I know, I feel the same way. But I'm sure you've noticed how many more troops there are in the city now, and they need our billets. I think it will just be temporary, if you get my drift. That's all for now. I'll let you know when I have further details."

As Smitty and Harry made their way back to the Atherstone Hotel through the square, they saw some kids climbing all over an American tank that was covered with camouflage netting. And there seemed to be more army trucks on the roads, bringing in supplies.

"I have a hunch something big is going on. . . . All of the American and Canadian armies coming in at once, but everything so hush-hush," Harry observed.

"On a clear day you can see straight over to Normandy," Smitty said.

"I'd have thought they'd be leaving from farther east, around Dover; it's a shorter crossing from there."

"And much more obvious to the Germans," Smitty added.

"I'm sure glad we're in the band—things could be so much worse for us."

"You're not kidding."

"Well, whatever it takes to end this abominable war."

Bournemouth, May 3, 1944 [excerpts]

My Darling Helen,

Well here I am up to my neck in packing, trying to stuff into kit bags the things collected over a period of eight months; and what a headache it is. I just received 900 cigarettes and two parcels of tin goods and candy from home which certainly doesn't make it any easier. . . .

We're moving to a station outside of Gloucester on Friday. Al [Smitty] *and I took a walk through the park tonight for one last look at the scenery and it certainly was beautiful. The tulip trees are out now . . . everybody is feeling sorry for themselves around here being posted to a station* [as opposed to boarding out in hotels]. *It's certainly hard to leave here though as you couldn't find a more beautiful spot* [than Bournemouth].

I believe we'll have other compensations to make up for our loss of living out; we should eat better for one thing. Talking about eating; four of us went out Sunday to scrounge a bacon and egg dinner off the nearest farmer we could find keeping chickens. This was in Riston near Warrington. We hit two and had three eggs and bacon. We were willing to pay them you know but they wouldn't take anything for it. It was the first time I'd ever done anything like that and will probably be the last time. I was hungry, but not that hungry.

Gloucester, May 5, 16, 1944 - Here I am writing from a barrack room on a station outside of Gloucester. We left Bournemouth this morning early and what a job I had carrying all my belongings! We didn't have to walk very far so I didn't get too weary, thank heavens.

We certainly are spoiled for this kind of a life. Cots without sheets after sleeping in feather beds are quite a let down. The mess hall is a good fifteen minute walk and the ablutions – wow! Well we're still travelling anyway; the 12-piece dance band is going up through York to play a dance tomorrow night and will probably be back sometime Sunday. We have no cupboard space whatsoever, only two pegs so I'll have to leave everything packed up. I hope nobody steals anything.

I know this travelling puts an awful strain on my disposition especially when we have to stand outside a railway station for two hours waiting for a transport that should have met us. We do enough waiting at strange stations without being treated like strangers at our own station. Well darling, that's the only gripe I'm going to put into this letter, I don't want to give you the impression that I'm browned off, because I'm not really.

Travelling is getting increasingly difficult by train as they are taking some of the runs off I see by the paper and we nearly always miss connections, due to trains being late.

No sooner did the dance band get back from a place near Bournemouth Saturday night than we had to pack off to Liverpool Sunday afternoon.

Cambridge, June 7, 1944 - We haven't had a minute to ourselves since we started this "Canada Day" tour last Sunday. . . .We arrived in Cambridge at noon Monday and there too the mayor treated us to luncheon. We also did a parade around town . . .another concert on one of those antiquated bandstands and also a dance.

When we awoke the next morning we were told the news that the whole world had been waiting to hear for months [i.e. about the D-Day invasion.][1]

June 12, 1944 - I hope you are getting at least some of the letters I have been writing. Now that the second front [i.e. in France] *has started maybe they'll let the mail through as usual.*

Love, Harry

Late on June 5, 1944, about 500 boats left from the quay at Poole, just west of Bournemouth, as well as over 6,000 naval vessels and approximately 11,000 aircraft from many other points along the southern coast of England, travelling across the English Channel to invade Europe. On D-Day, June 6, the 156,000 Allied troops, including 14,000 Canadians, landed on the French beaches at Normandy for what was called Operation Overlord. The invasion was the result of years of training and practice, under utmost secrecy, with elaborate camouflaging and false military exercises designed to deceive the enemy as to the actual plans.

Upon landing, over 4,000 were killed, including about 340 Canadians. Throughout the summer, the

---

1 Harry was reluctant to refer directly to D-Day because of the military censors and the printed caption that was at the bottom of many of his letters: *"Think—Any reference to shipping or troop movements will result in the delay or mutilation of this letter."*

remaining troops pushed deeper inland, steadily unsettling the German stronghold.

Even though Harry was still writing faithfully, Helen hadn't received a letter from him for about a month, possibly due to military resources being diverted to the second front.

Toronto, June 7, 1944 [excerpt]

Darling Harry,

I've just been sitting here looking at old pictures and reading old letters, and realize that after not seeing you for over ten months, I still think just as much or more of you honey. I'll be so happy when I receive a letter from you again. I've waited only two days longer than three weeks, but oh! it seems months for me. Surely it will be coming through soon.

I heard the big news [about D-Day] *about seven o'clock yesterday morning, and I just couldn't sleep after that. There just wasn't anything else on the radio all day. They told us the news was received very quietly in London. The general comment was "That's good". I phoned your Mother about ten and she didn't even know about it; she said they didn't have the radio on before they went to bed. When I went to work yesterday afternoon the men were talking about it and kept us back from our work for an hour or so. We didn't hear the King's speech at three.*

Kay just got another letter from her Merchant Marine. She waited five months for the one before that and told me last night that I might have to wait that long. I said I wouldn't write then but she assured me I would.

I've been sitting here a long time writing this darling but enjoy doing it if I know you are receiving them. As you will conclude from what I've said, I'm still missing you and loving you and will until I can have you with me again, and always after that.

Bye, Love and kisses, Helen

* * *

In 1941 the British cracked the secret German code machine called Enigma. They were able to intercept German radio signals and knew in advance what actions the Germans were planning.

Some historians maintain that Prime Minister Winston Churchill knew ahead of time that the Luftwaffe were planning to bomb the city of Coventry and destroy its fourteenth-century cathedral on November 13, 1940, but decided not to do anything about it for fear that the Germans would find out that the British had broken the code. As a result, not only was the cathedral bombed, but around that time several munitions factories and buildings in the city were also destroyed, resulting in many civilian casualties. Some believe Coventry was sacrificed "for the greater good."

This information was not known at the time, but came to light in the 1970s, long after the war had ended.

* * *

RCAF band playing in the open air

Continuing on its tour of the English Midlands, the RCAF band spent a weekend in June 1944 in Coventry, where it played several concerts, including one for the British Royal Air Force Sports Day in the middle of a track while a Spitfire pilot put on an aerial show for the crowd.

Afterward, Smitty and Harry made their way to their billet on the outskirts of town.

"Was it my imagination, or was that pilot using us as a target?" asked Harry.

"Yeah, he was diving right at us for about fifteen minutes—I think he forgot that we weren't the enemy," said Smitty.

"He certainly was skilful, pulling out of a dive in the nick of time and just skimming the trees. I guess after all those missions to the continent, this would be child's play." They knocked on the door of a tiny cottage that had a large tin hut in the backyard.

"Good afternoon, boys, come on in," said an older gentleman. "I'm Mike and this is my wife Betty."

"Thanks for having us. You people here have had quite a time of it," said Smitty. "The downtown is pretty much destroyed."

"Aye, we're lucky to be alive," he said. "The Gerries rained down on us steadily for three months. I don't think the wife and I took our clothes off that whole time, what with running

Love in the Air

out back to the bomb shelter at all hours of the day and night. It will take a long time for us to rebuild, but things are looking up now that the second front has started. Here, we'll show you to your room."

After they deposited their kit bags, Harry and Smitty headed back downtown. They walked along to the site of the bombed-out medieval cathedral, to see for themselves the horrific destruction.

"Nothing left but the tower, spire, and part of a wall," Smitty said solemnly as they looked at what used to be the cathedral's interior, now a pile of rubble. "The futility of war—a building that had lasted for 700 years, only to be destroyed in a single day."

"I suppose we've done an equal amount of damage on their side," Harry remarked. Smitty nodded.

"It was beautiful inside," said a grey-haired woman, coming over to them. "Ornately carved arches on both sides of the centre aisle. Would you boys like some tea?"

"Sure. Thanks."

"Where are you from?"

"Toronto," Smitty replied.

"Well, this tea wagon was donated to us by the citizens of Guelph after the Blitz," she said.

"No kidding, that's just sixty miles west of where we live," Harry observed.

"Help has been pouring in from all over, but I doubt our city will ever be the same. . . . However, it did bring us all together; we spent so much time in the communal shelters during the bombings." The woman managed a feeble smile and began pouring their tea.

Harry let out a small sigh. "Let's all pray that the war will be over by the end of summer."

Coventry, June 20, 1944

My Dearest Helen,

We are just waiting for a transport to take us back to our station which is just 25 miles from here. We had a very nice weekend in Coventry although we were quite busy yesterday. We played two – 2 hour concerts in the park there and on Saturday we played all afternoon for an RAF Sports day. The whole band was billeted out to different homes and Al and I went together to a very nice couple's place on the outskirts of town.

Needless to say, the downtown area is knocked about quite a bit. I noticed Woolworths and J. Lyons are still doing business in a very modest way in a corrugated tin garage. The Cathedral was burnt out by incendiaries and although the steeple is still standing, the inside is filled with rubble. I noticed a tea wagon that was donated to the city from the citizens of Guelph. They must have had quite a time while it lasted as these people didn't take their clothes off for three months.

We got quite a thrill on Saturday at the park. We were playing out in the middle of the track and a Spitfire was scheduled to put on a show for the crowd. That part was all right but the pilot used us as a target and dived at us for about 15 minutes. I was glad when it was over as he just skimmed the trees when he pulled out of a dive at an incredible speed.

Well we arrived back here after a charming truck ride of about an hour's duration and learning we had to play a dance tonight. I'm not getting stale or anything but I sure would like a leave.

Well, darling, there's not much news around here. It looks like I wrote that down too soon as Steve just told us we were going up to Scotland tomorrow. It's one of our longest trips but anything is better than hanging around here I guess. So I'll be writing to you from Glasgow probably.

All my love sweet. Harry.

* * *

The German Luftwaffe dropped a wide range of bombs on England over the course of the war. By June 13, 1944, they had developed two new weapons. The V-1, nicknamed a "buzz bomb" or "doodlebug," was a small pilotless aircraft that was dropped by a plane. Carrying one tonne of explosives and travelling at 400 mph, its range was about 200 miles. The V-2 was a rocket, flying independently, that was launched from northern France and travelled at 2,400 mph. The "V" stood for "Vergeltungswaffe," or "vengeance weapon."

During June 1944, possibly in retaliation for the D-Day invasion by the Allies, there was a barrage of bombing on London. After their tour to Scotland, the RCAF No. 3 Personnel Reception Centre Band was in the city at the BBC Studios cutting records that would be broadcast for Allied troops on the continent over the ACF Radio Network.

By the time they got to their fifth piece that day, "Long Ago and Far Away" by Ira Gershwin and Jerome Kern, Steve, their bandmaster, was at his wits' end.

"You guys are playing well but we need to do a retake—the technicians say they can hear the sirens and explosions in the background. I guess the soundproofing in this studio isn't as good as the blackout curtains. We'll take it one more time from the top and see if we can get a clean take. Maybe the Gerries will give us a break for five minutes."

"As long as we can hear those doodlebugs, we're okay, but as soon as you don't hear them, look out, they're going into a nosedive," Harry whispered to Ossie.

No sooner did they sound the last note than there was an explosion in what seemed to be the next building. The BBC recording technicians ran to the shelter, while the musicians fell over themselves looking for cover. Harry and Ossie dove under the grand piano, where they stayed huddled together for what seemed like hours. Nobody moved until they heard the all-clear siren.

RCAF dance band, pianist Al Smith on left, saxophonist Harry Culley, second from right

London, June 30, 1944

Dearest Helen,

Well Darling, I promised to tell you about our London trip. We got through the five records without too many bumps on our part. There was an almost continuous alert on during the process but we were in a pretty safe spot under the BBC

House. The records are for the forces overseas so you won't be able to hear them. I went to one Prom concert and Myra Hess played a concerto but I really didn't enjoy it as there were several distractions during the program. [i.e. bombs exploding.]

I was very uneasy last night when one passed very low overhead. I might say I was scared, but so was everyone. Smitty practically lived in the shelter and began to look quite green this morning. Lucky we didn't have to stay any longer than three days [in London.] *It's very hard on the nerves with sirens going on at all hours of the day and night. So much for that!*

I can tell you what one [a buzz bomb] *sounds like. Just imagine the biggest truck you've ever seen going up a street like Winnett* [the street where Helen lives in Toronto]. *There'd be quite a vibration in the houses. Only two came over London yesterday, so they must be destroying more bases every day* [i.e. the Allies must be destroying the German bases in Europe where the bombs originated.]

We had to play a broadcast, quiet so far. We're going to rehearse a bit tomorrow and I hope it's not raining because there's no roof on the only place we can get. It was blown off recently by a near hit.

All my love, Harry

| |
Songs of Love—But Not for Me

They're writing songs of love—but not for me
A lucky star's above—but not for me
With love to lead the way I've found more clouds of gray
Than any Russian play could guarantee

"But Not for Me," lyrics by Ira Gershwin,
music by George Gershwin

Harry's younger brother Ross, aged twenty-two, was about to
marry his high school sweetheart Elaine, aged eighteen, whom
he'd been dating for several years. Helen was looking forward
to their wedding, but knew she would have mixed emotions
once she got there, not knowing if she could keep her envy
at bay.

As she entered the church, she spotted Harry's parents as
well as Ross driving up. She wished them well then went to
the groom's side of the church, where she sat behind Harry's
grandparents. They turned around and invited her to join
them, and Grandma Culley commented on how much everyone
thought Helen looked like Betty, Harry's cousin who lived in
New York City. Helen smiled weakly at this and at all of the

relatives sitting around her and tried to remain composed, but it wasn't easy. She kept thinking about how she wished that she and Harry were getting married and that it had been such a long time since she'd heard from him. Why was he being so silent? It didn't help matters when some people suggested all the other things that might be going on with him, such as seeing other women. She seemed to need his reassurance regularly, especially when he was so far away.

Hearing the organ music begin and turning to watch Elaine come up the aisle, Helen vowed to put her feelings aside for the time being and be happy for the young couple.

Toronto, June 17, 1944

Darling Harry,

I hardly know where to start in telling you about everything. My mind is in such a state of confusion just now. Anyway, it turned out to be a perfect day . . .

Elaine looked so charming as she walked up. Really I think I was almost as excited as she was. The ceremony wasn't very long; Gordon Darling sang during the signing of the register. I'm thinking so many things in between these sentences but I can't seem to explain them to you. They were gone by the time we got out of the church. I stayed with your Grandmother and she made me acquainted with more of your relatives, who all passed the remark that they thought I was Betty sitting there; I resemble her so much. Art said I could consider that quite a compliment. I met Mrs. McGuire too, her two boys are over there [fighting in Europe] *and she hasn't heard from them for some time. We rode up to the Alexandra Palace; your Grandfather was muttering away to himself, but seemed to be enjoying everything. She* [Grandmother Culley] *keeps nudging him and he knows what to do next. She was talking about the two of you* [i.e. Harry Jr. and Ross] *all the way up. We had to wait about half an hour for the bridal party to arrive then we filed into the reception room.*

When I offered my best wishes to Elaine, she thanked me and said "Don't you wish this was you standing here?" My feelings at that I didn't express. They served punch, dainty sandwiches, cookies and ice cream and the wedding cake. The photographer was there to snap her when she was cutting it. I asked Mrs. Ackerman [Elaine's mother] *if she would save a piece to send to you and she said she would give it to your Mother. Your Dad, Art and members of the band and Navy were absent for a short while* [perhaps having a drink] *then when they came down from upstairs, the minister gave the toast to the bride, and before the best man toasted the groom he read your cable, also Billie Haye's which I thought was a very nice gesture. Oh! you were so close then dearest. Is there any reason why the afternoon was a bit difficult for me? I'm just a funny person, I guess. Ross was slightly nervous but responded very well. . .*

We saw all her gifts last night, and they were lovely. Mine wasn't duplicated [Helen gave them a casserole dish], *but she got four coffee silexes. The only thing they said they needed was a tea kettle.*

It has been pretty terrible over there the last few days. How many times those people must wonder how long it is going to last. Were you anywhere near the bombed area? It isn't very safe there right now.

Well, darling, I'm going to lie down for awhile. Maybe you know how much I missed you today. Did you think of them [Ross and Elaine] *at three (nine your time)? I must love you so very much honey or I wouldn't feel "like this" tonight.*

So long dear. Yours always, Helen xxx

England, June 12, 1944

My Darling Helen,

We have just completed our tour of the eastern provinces and believe me I'm plenty glad. Ceremonies might impress the people over there but it's a pain in the neck to me.

I'm terribly sorry about the mail situation, darling, but there's nothing I can do about it. Everybody is complaining at home about not getting letters for over a month even. I'm keeping my promise; I mean the one I made about writing more often and when you do get them you will realize that. Say, what do I have to say to convince you that I love you? I'm glad you don't listen to those people you are living with. What a pair of warped minds they must have!

I was surprised to hear that Ross is getting married and will already be in that state when you receive this. I don't blame him a bit and my only wish is that it could have been a double wedding. Don't you?

We'll be on the road again this week-end. There
always seems to be some place we haven't been to.
I don't mind it a bit though especially on week-
ends because I wouldn't know what to do with
myself around here.

Goodbye for now sweetheart.

All my love, Harry

* * *

During the Second World War, families tried to carry on as usual without loved ones. For those without vehicles, getting out of the city presented a challenge during the hot summer months. Two popular excursions at the time were taking the ferry to the Toronto Islands and going by boat on Lake Ontario to Niagara Falls.

The Cayuga steamship travelled daily between Toronto and Queenston Heights on the Niagara Peninsula throughout the 1940s. The trip took approximately two hours, depending on the weather. The passengers passed the time by viewing the scenery and having refreshments, and on the way back, enjoying evening entertainment.

Reluctantly, Helen woke up at 6 a.m. when her alarm went off. She'd worked until 12:30 a.m. the night before, on the evening shift, and knew she would be tired, but she reasoned that the summer was almost half over and she might not get another opportunity to visit Niagara Falls. She'd been in the east three years now and hadn't made the trip yet, so when Ida suggested the outing, she jumped at the chance. Plus, she thought the fresh air would do her good.

Looking out her window as she got dressed, she thought it was a bit cloudy outside and might rain, but they'd made their plans, so she quickly ate some cereal and toast and was out the door and down at the docks by 7:45 a.m. to meet Harry's mother.

They sat out on the lower deck by the railing so that they could see the water, but went inside when it got too windy.

"I guess you and the boys have made this trip many times," said Helen.

"Yes, we usually tried to go at least once a season; Harry and Ross really got a kick out of it. We'd usually do something different each time we went, like go out on the Maid of the Mist boat below the falls, or get our photos taken," Ida replied.

The sun gradually came out and the weather was totally clear by the time they reached Queenston. Quite a crowd had gathered and they had to stand up in the buses that took them to the falls.

After eating their picnic lunch of salmon sandwiches, tea, and cake in the park, they went over to the falls and gazed at the water rushing down to the gorge, marvelling at its power and breathing in the mistiness of the air. Standing silently, they were lost in their own thoughts for several minutes. Then they wandered around the shops, buying souvenirs and postcards to send to Harry.

"Oh, I forgot to bring my pen with me. Do you have one, Ida?" Helen asked her.

"No, I'm afraid not, dear."

"Oh well, I guess I'll send them when I get home; he's always sending me postcards of all the beautiful places he's been, so now it's my turn."

After supper at the Foxhead Inn in Niagara Falls, they caught the 6:30 p.m. bus back to Queenston. A storm was brewing and fortunately they were on the boat before it hit.

The music started up on the main deck, and as the passengers went over to the dance floor, Helen watched them dreamily, thinking about how she wished Harry were there to hold her tight and whisper lovingly in her ear while dancing. When the band played "Night and Day," she thought about the words and how their meaning fit her feelings exactly: "Whether near to me or far, it's no matter, darling, where you are, I think of you day and night." Outside, the rain teemed down and the lightning flashed off in the distance. The dramatic weather seemed to reflect her inner state—tumultuous emotions that only Harry could calm.

To steady herself, she stopped at the refreshment stand to buy a couple of cups of coffee and brought them back to Ida without spilling them, despite the roughness of the water.

It was close to midnight by the time they reached Toronto.

Toronto, July 2 – Aug. 23, 1944 [excerpts]

My Darling Harry:

Well we got back all right last night honey, but we were both very tired. I could hardly keep my eyes open on the streetcar. Your Mother wanted me to come up for the night, but I thought it best to come home.

We arrived there [at Niagara Falls] *about 11:30 a.m. and your Mother was starved so we went to the park and had our lunch, which she brought, then we walked around the grounds and gazed at the Falls. They are beautiful and fascinating aren't they? It's impossible to go near them on the Canadian side now and they're even more terrific there. You could go further than the Park Restaurant at one time couldn't you? I wandered down that far by myself after we'd had a rest in the park. We should have brought our birth certificates, then we could have gone across to the American side.*

I finished my film and tried to get another, but couldn't, so only have three, and maybe they won't turn out. The afternoon wasn't long at all; we had supper at the Foxhead Inn, and began queuing up for the bus about 6:30 p.m. and had an hour's wait, but we were on first, and enjoyed the ride back. The boat was late in and didn't leave until 9:20 p.m. We parked ourselves on the upper deck – it was nice until the storm came up. I got a bit dizzy so walked around and watched them dance. It didn't last very long though, so we went out again. It was almost twelve when we docked. We both enjoyed the day; I would have been more lonesome for you if she [Ida] *hadn't been with me. You were in my thoughts darling.*

Harry I just had a nice letter from Mary Gibson [Helen's friend in the CWACs], *and do you know what? She said your band was there* [in England] *to greet them along with other Air Force person-nel. She recognized you too, and said it was so nice to see a familiar face so soon, but she was not in a position to speak to you, otherwise she says, "I could have given him first hand news about his fiancée but I imagine you look after that pretty well yourself". She has seen her Norman, who was just stationed ten miles away —also her sister. She's very busy, but had a bicycle so is seeing the countryside. She might be stationed at the hospital where you were playing.*

Well honey, guess I better go now, as it's nearly time to get ready for work and I'll have to dig out my rubbers and umbrella.

So long sweetheart.

All my love and kisses, Helen.

July 21, Aug. 12, 1944 [excerpts]

My Dearest Darling Helen,

Just received your very romantic post cards from Niagara Falls. How I wish I could have been with you dearest. I know just how tiresome that trip is too, especially when it's hot!! Mother's air letter came this morning dated 24th, exactly a week, isn't that terrific!

. . . I received your five letters up until August 2 to-day and also the snaps sweetheart!! I'd like to give you a great big kiss for sending them. Those high cheek bones of yours do things to me. Pardon me for being nosey, but isn't that the same dress you wore last summer? Mother's looking well, isn't she?. . .

All my love, angel. Harry.

Helen Reeder and Ida Culley at Niagara Falls

* * *

"I've never been in a hospital before, imagine that," said Helen.

"I was in one only once, when I had scarlet fever as a child," said Ida. "Both boys were born at home."

"Even when my brother spilled hot gravy all over me and I was burned badly, the doctor came to the farm and bandaged me up," Helen added.

The two were on their way to the Christie Street Veterans' Hospital to visit a young man Helen knew from Saskatchewan.[1]

"Do you have his room number, Helen?" asked Ida.

"Yes, Florence gave it to me," Helen replied, fishing it out of her pocket.

"What did you say happened to him?"

"Well, Florence wrote to tell me her brother Ray had been wounded in the Italian campaign and was sent here shortly afterward. I think his arm was badly damaged. He hasn't had any visitors as he doesn't know anyone in Toronto, so she asked me to go to see him," Helen said.

Walking down the long corridor, they passed by rooms where wounded soldiers rested in beds, some paralyzed, some with no arms or legs. Helen was shocked at the sight and couldn't help worrying about Harry, thankful that he was in a non-combat role, but realizing that with one step the wrong way at the wrong time, he could be in here.

A kindly nurse ushered them to the lounge, where Ray was sitting up, with a bandaged arm.

"Ray, it's Helen from Thaxted, and this is my fiancé's mother, Ida Culley," Helen explained. "Florence wanted us to come and see you. How are you?"

Ray smiled. "Not too bad considering."

"From what Florence said, it's amazing that you're alive," Helen said.

"Yes, the Gerries rained down pretty hard on us. I jumped out of the way just in the nick of time. My buddy wasn't so lucky."

---

1   During the Second World War so many injured soldiers came to the Christie Street Veterans' Hospital (also known as the Military Orthopedic Hospital) that it became overcrowded. As a result, in 1948 the new Sunnybrook Hospital opened to care for veterans.

"I'm so sorry. Is there anything we can do for you?" Helen asked.

"No, thanks, they're treating me pretty well here. How are things in Saskatchewan?"

"Fine, I guess. I'm working in Toronto now at the TTC, not far from here."

"I'll leave you two to talk," Ida said, spotting a piano on the other side. She made her way over, and as she started to play, the patients sitting around the room began perking up.

"Where is your fiancé stationed?" Ray asked.

"Harry's pretty safe—he's down in Bournemouth most of the time, but they do go to London regularly, so I worry when he's there."

"He's one of the fortunate ones."

The two sat in silence for a moment.

"Do you have a girlfriend?" Helen asked.

Ray smiled. "Yes, Rose back home, if she's still waiting for me."

"Oh, I'm sure she'll be so happy to see you again."

Helen could hear Ida playing "An Hour Never Passes" and she grew quiet for a little while as she listened to the beautiful melody and lyrics: "But I keep recalling those old happy times, without my prayer for you in each lonely sigh, an hour never passes by." They were so true. She thought about Harry constantly and knew she would be beside herself if anything ever happened to him.

Toronto, July 9 - Sept. 13, 1944 [excerpts]

My Darling Harry,

Last night the two of us went to the Hospital. Ray was sitting on the sofa so we sat with him for a few minutes then your Mother played and we walked down with him to see the first part of an entertainment show, left around nine and I went home with her for an hour or so. He was wounded

Love in the Air

badly, but his arm is all right. He seems very cheerful and isn't suffering much now.

. . . Are you still up in Glasgow? You should like going there; at least it's safe anyway. I bet you wouldn't get over that episode in London for a few days. If you were actually confronted with it all the time, you would be accustomed to it like the boys in the fighting lines. I don't know how they can have any nerves at all. Those robots [i.e. V-1 and V-2 pilotless rockets] *are the most terrible menace yet; they* [the Allies] *seem to be doing all in their power to combat them though. I hope you don't have to go back* [to London] *for awhile. Those poor people go through so much.*

On the news this morning there were reports of more bombings on the south coast – well, that starts me wondering. It's impossible to keep up with current events the way our troops are pro-gressing now – it's great.

Mrs. Roosevelt and Mrs. Churchill just spoke on the air; thanking Canadians for their hospitality and speaking words of encouragement in both English and French.[2] There will be much excite-ment at Quebec this week. So far, their plans have been carried out – if only the final phases don't last too long.

My days are filled with just little things, and I'm not in a position to see something different as you are, although there is much in this city I have

---

2   The Second Quebec Conference involving Winston Churchill, Franklin D. Roosevelt, and Mackenzie King took place in Quebec City from September 12 to 16, 1944, to develop the Morgenthau Plan for post-war Germany and the Hyde Park Agreement.

Joanne Culley

yet to see. I know you have influenced me in my interests, outlook and naturally, my thoughts — that fact just came to me dear.

Have you heard that song "An Hour Never Passes?" – it's nice.

So long sweetheart.

All my love and kisses, Helen

Love in the Air

12

Things Are Looking Up

I cover the waterfront
I'm watching the sea
Will the one I love
Be coming back to me

"I Cover the Waterfront," lyrics by Edward
Heyman, music by Johnny Green

After being away for four months, the band was finally back
in Bournemouth. They had been ordered to leave the city in
advance of D-Day on June 6 to make room for the incoming troops.

Getting off the train, they carried their kit bags through
streets overflowing with rhododendrons to the Knights of
Columbus, their temporary quarters. Each claiming a cot, they
draped their belongings around their own sleeping spots.

RCAF band members on a railway bridge, Harry Culley on right

"It's good to be back in the most beautiful place on earth," Harry said.

"Why don't we go out and celebrate?" Ossie suggested.

"What did you have in mind?"

"Let's take all our leave rations and hit the shops over in Boscombe."[1]

"Great idea!"

Several of them headed down to the main-street butcher, and each bought two-inch-thick beefsteaks—twice the civilian ration for a week—then bought milk and Hovis loaves at the grocer's.

"Let's go back and get the cook to prepare this for us," Ossie said.

"What a lift a bottle of milk can give you after being deprived of it for so long," Harry commented on their way back after drinking one of the two quarts he had bought. "I feel like a million, no kidding."

After handing over their groceries to the cook, they relaxed at the mess tables. Soon, dinner was served.

---

1   Boscombe is a suburb of Bournemouth to the east.

"This is the most delicious steak I've ever tasted," Smitty said with his mouth full, savouring every bite.

"A good meal can sure boost the morale," Harry replied.

"So, how much do you weigh now?"

"One hundred forty-nine pounds, with my boots on—the most I've ever weighed in my life."

"Well, we all should get fatter now that we're back in Bournemouth."

"I guess we better check the newspapers and see if we can find more permanent accommodations," Harry said, pushing his plate away.

"I'm way ahead of you there," chimed in Smitty. "I picked up a *Bournemouth Times* at the train station. But there doesn't seem to be much available—only rooms in the suburbs, which would mean standing in queues for hours and taking the bus four times a day, to get to our rehearsals and shows."

"I guess we'll have to put an ad in ourselves if we're to find anything half decent."

"How about we do that tomorrow? It's too nice a day to waste. Look at that view—the channel is beckoning," said Smitty.

"You're on—let's go down to the beach."

As they walked down the Upper Cliff Road, they noticed that the barbed wire had been lifted from the beach so they could walk along the two miles of sand toward what was left of the Bournemouth pier. They could see the white cliffs of the Isle of Wight off in the distance.

"It's hard to believe all those ships left from here," mused Harry.

"Yeah, that newsreel showed thousands of them going over to Normandy. It seems that many of them left from Poole and Weymouth, just over there." Smitty pointed farther west along the coast.

"Too bad we weren't here to witness it all," Harry said. "Do you ever feel guilty that we aren't fighting on the front lines?"

"Sometimes. I did get rifle training, but my eyesight was poor and when they knew I could play an instrument, they assigned me to the band," replied Smitty.

"I didn't even try for combat duty. I knew my mother would have had a fit; as it was, she didn't want me to join up. My parents had just returned from England before the war started when the tensions were brewing. My being in the band was the most she could tolerate."

"If we had gone to the continent, chances are you and I wouldn't be having this conversation right now."

As they got closer to the Pavilion near downtown Bournemouth, they found a spot on the beach and joined the other sunbathers. They noticed a couple of scantily clad women talking briefly to some soldiers in deck chairs, then moving on to another group farther down.

"I suppose those are 'ladies of the day,' as opposed to 'ladies of the night,'" Smitty observed.

"Too bad they have to do that, but I guess the war has been devastating for a lot of people, ruining their livelihoods and taking away husbands," said Harry.

"It's tempting, but I'd rather wait until I meet someone I love. Plus, there's less chance of disease," Smitty remarked.

"A lot of the guys go for it, especially the ones heading to the front," added Harry.

The two fell silent for a while, watching the waves crash in.

"Outside of those planes passing overhead and the almost continuous artillery practice, you'd hardly know there was a war on," Harry said after a few moments.

"Here, have a cigar—I've been saving them up for just this moment. To our safe arrival back in Bournemouth and to the steady advance of the second front." Smitty lit both their smokes.

"Here's to all those brave souls who crossed the channel and sacrificed their lives for us," Harry said, lifting his cigar.

Bournemouth, Sept. 7, 1944

My Darling Helen,

I hope you will have more luck in finding a room than we are darling . . . We're going to see about some furnished flats tomorrow and hope we have more luck.

I played a job in Boscombe last night (a suburb of Bournemouth) and I was the only sax with three rhythm. Boy did I sweat! I'm working tomorrow night if I can contact the man. By the way I played alto and can still get a good tone on it so the tenor hasn't done it any harm. I'm afraid I smashed up the tenor a bit when I threw it on the floor one night; it works with a couple of elastics though.

Well our leave is almost over – it seemed very short really . . . I spend my leisure time walking through the gardens here and along the sea shore when it isn't too cool. That's about all there is to do outside of shows and dances. I think we'll be going to London in a couple of weeks for nine days to relieve the #1 band. The authorities seem to agree that London is now safe from any attack the enemy might think up. I think the Germans will be in for an even greater ordeal when the air force really starts to work on them.

Sept. 13, 1944 - I haven't received a letter from you this week, I hope you're not mad at me angel or are you busy looking for a room? Al and I found one in Winton, 10 minutes on a bus from the Square with a nice old lady who can't seem to do enough for us. The room is very nice with two single beds and ridiculously cheap – 28 shillings a week with breakfast and dinner, we'll have to rustle up our own supper at night as she's working until 8:30 p.m. every week day. She didn't want to take anything for the room while we were travelling but we talked her into taking a shilling every day we were on the road. One of the chaps got talking to an old lady who wouldn't let him pay a cent for her room – how about that!

Well darling, we're going up to Liverpool tomorrow morning but will be back here Saturday night to play an officer's dance and church parade Sunday; rather a busy weekend. We're moving into our room on Monday and I think we'll be very comfortable. We hired a taxi this afternoon to take our kit up and what a load it was.

Al and I spent a very enjoyable evening just sitting on the sand watching the waves break while we smoked a cigar. Great life eh? Now that we're in the money again it puts a new light on things in general. Now that I've saved £200 I'm going to do all I can to save £300.

We've been doing a little rehearsing this week on some new music; we're playing a show at the Regent theatre Sunday night for the boys [i.e. the American, British and Canadian troops stationed in Bournemouth.]

Well, sweetheart, I'm getting a little sleepy and all the other boys are in bed. It's another day closer to the end of the war and you angel; that's how I look at it. Good night sweetheart.

All my love forever. Harry

*RCAF band members having a break on a station,
with Nissen huts in the background*

In the fall of 1944, the band took another tour through the Midlands to raise money for the war in the Victory Loan bond drive. While playing concerts and dances in the officers' mess at night, and parades in nearby towns during the day, the musicians stayed in Nissen corrugated steel huts on the stations. These structures were common during the war, as they could be put up and taken down quickly and provided accommodation efficiently. They were also used for other purposes, such as storing munitions. Sometimes their roofs would be covered with earth and grass so that they would be camouflaged from enemy planes. However, they were quite cold and drafty, and the bandmates were feeling it as the weather started to take a turn for the worse.

"Barracks life is pretty boring; all we have to do is listen to the rain teeming on the roof," Smitty complained as he laid back on his cot, pulling the thin, scratchy army-issue wool blanket over him.

"I know, we've certainly been spoiled living out in comfortable homes and being doted on by older women," said Harry.

"So Mrs. Hart treats you well?" asked Bill.

"You bet. She gets home from work at 8:30 p.m., then she makes us tea and sandwiches, and we're up yammering away till about 10 p.m. or 11 p.m.," replied Smitty.

"She looks after us like a Trojan—she even does our laundry and irons our shirts," Harry added.

"You guys certainly lucked out—it's pretty much every man for himself back at the Atherstone Hotel, Bournemouth's finest," grumbled Bill.

"Well, it makes up for our lack of female affection," said Harry. "Which reminds me, I should get started on a letter to Helen." He dug into his kit bag for his pen, ink, and airmail form.

"You two lovebirds should do what Les and his girlfriend do," said Bill.

"What's that?" Harry inquired. "Or dare I ask?"

"At a predetermined time, they both go into dark rooms, close their eyes, and concentrate hard on the other one, who's on the opposite side of the Atlantic, and they claim they can communicate to each other through their minds," Bill explained.

Harry lit a cigarette and chuckled. "They sound like nut-cases to me. Good thing they found each other."

"Did you hear about the shenanigans Joe was up to the other night?" asked Smitty. "He brought one of the WAAFs back to his room at the Atherstone, and when his buddies got wind of it, they set up a gramophone outside and played the record his girlfriend back home had made of her singing 'O Promise Me' at top volume, to remind him of his loyalties. Boy, was he mad."

They all laughed at that one.

"Come to think of it, I haven't had a letter from Helen's cousin Georgie yet," Bill said.

"Weren't you supposed to write her first?" Harry asked.

"Let's see her picture again. . . . Hmmm . . . she's a pretty good-looker," Bill remarked. "Do you have her address?"

"Somewhere, I think in one of the letters from a few months ago. Here's a blank airmail—you get started and I'll look for it."

"Do you carry those love letters around with you every-where you go?" Bill asked.

"Yeah, so, what's it to you?" Harry replied.

"Just wondering, that's all. No offense," Bill said.

"Harry's sensitive when it comes to Helen," Smitty kidded him.

"It's getting cold in here. Does anyone know how to work the stove?" Harry asked, changing the subject.

"I could try," Smitty offered, taking out his lighter and flick-ing it inside the heater. "I don't know why it's not catching."

"Where's Jonesy? He's good at fixing things."

"Did I hear someone call my name?" Jonesy said as he entered the hut, dripping wet.

"We can't get this stove to go and we're freezing to death in here," Smitty replied.

"Maybe the chimney's plugged up; I'll go have a look." After checking the stove, Jonesy grabbed a broom, went back outside, and climbed on the roof. He poked the handle down the chimney, and lo and behold, a heap of soot came pouring out the other end.

Gloucester, Wed. Oct. 18, 1944

My Darling Helen,

Just a few lines to let you know I am keeping well and hope you are too. We've had so much rain up here that we're all beginning to feel like ducks and we'll be here all week and I'm sure I don't know why because all we're doing is playing a dance on Saturday night. . . .

Bill is writing to Georgie across from me and is having quite a time in the process. He's been going to write for months but doesn't know what to put in the letter. I'm sure I can't help him much. I have a tough enough time with my own!

I've just been reading your letters over again darling, you see our mail is being forwarded on Saturday so I'll just have to wait patiently until then to hear how you spent your holidays. I hope you had decent weather as that helps a lot doesn't it? Did you take any snaps? I hate to keep bugging you about that but you know how I like to get them.

It's very miserable here though, all one has for entertainment is drinking and I'm trying awfully hard not to do too much! Believe me I am. xx

Smitty and I went to the Monk's Retreat last night. You go down a flight of stairs to get in and it's about 300 years old. It seems the monks had a tunnel from the Gloucester Cathedral to this underground chamber and they stored their beer there. Hence the name Retreat.

Well sweetheart, how are you getting on? I wish I could see you tonight and tell you just how much I love you. I'll bet it would be nice at the Old Mill [restaurant in Toronto] *tonight, just the two of us. I just wonder if you dream about us as much as I do angel.*

What a drab existence barrack life is compared to the way we are living. We have two little stoves in the hut which Jonesy our discipe [disciplinarian] *takes the greatest joy in keeping alight. Last night one of them refused to keep going so we figured the chimney (a pipe) was plugged with soot. It was teeming rain but that didn't stop Jonesy from climbing on the roof and poking a broom down the chimney and getting half a pail of soot out of it. It went after that believe me. What language he called that stove! He sure is big hearted though and we all like him.*

Well, darling, I've rambled on about myself as usual but I guess you like to know what I'm doing with myself. I sure like to know how you are doing. How long, Oh Lord, how long!

Must close now sweetheart, much as I hate to. I don't like hurrying away, especially from you, you know that! angel. I'd like to hold you in my arms and tell you everything I've been thinking while I've been writing this.

All my love honey. Harry.

13
Victory Loan

Someday I'll meet you again
Tell me where, tell me when
Someday I'll meet you again
And I'm yours until then

"Someday I'll Meet You Again," by the Ink Spots

Helen and her friends from work, Connie and Kay, were looking forward to Wednesday night—the Toronto Transportation Commission's Victory Loan fundraiser at the popular Savarin Restaurant and Tavern in downtown Toronto. Fortunately, the young women were able to arrange their shifts so they could be off that evening.

Money was still needed for the war effort, especially now that the tide was turning for the Allies with their troops moving steadily through Europe.

The dining room was filled with brightly coloured streamers as about 250 people made their way to their tables.

"My, you'd think it was already Victory Day the way this room is decorated," Connie commented.

"Well, the news the last few days is good, with Canadians and Americans making significant headway," said Helen.

"It won't be long now," said Kay as they squeezed through the crowd to find a spot.

"Mind if we join you?" Helen asked the group sitting at one of the tables.

"Not at all, these seats are vacant."

"Where are you girls from?" Helen asked.

"Head Office. What about you?"

"We're in the Motor Traffic Division at Davenport and Bathurst," she said.

"I'm Lillian, and this is Mary."

As everyone introduced themselves, Helen noted how smart they all looked, a little different from the more casual get-togethers they'd had when she'd worked at the Department of Munitions and Supply in Ottawa.

"I think our bosses let us come because our department is working so hard on the drive—we went over the top last night," said Connie. "Frank in our department sold $5,000[1] worth of bonds in two days to the drivers and the other staff."

"And in our spare time we've been booking charter buses for the military bands to give fundraising concerts around the province," said Helen.

"So, do any of you have boyfriends overseas?" asked Lillian as she lit a cigarette.

"Helen's fiancé is in England, and my boyfriend is on the continent—I'm not sure where at this point; I haven't heard from him in a while," said Connie.

"You know, I just heard the other day that 20,000 Canadians have taken English brides, and that it's only about one in a hundred fellows who don't go out on dates, even if they have girlfriends and wives," said Lillian.

---

1   Worth about $75,000 in today's currency

"Oh, don't listen to her, Helen and Connie. I'm sure most of the men are true to their sweethearts back home," Kay quickly countered.

"Shh—the head commissioner's about to speak," said Connie.

"Welcome, ladies and gentlemen. Glad to see you all here tonight. We're pleased at the good news coming to us from Europe; it won't be long now until we're victorious, especially if we continue to do our part here at home to support our boys in the forces. The Toronto Transportation Commission is doing all we can to raise money to ensure triumph—we'll be sending around a memo next week with plans outlining scheduling for V-Day when that happy day arrives. In the meantime, we have a full evening ahead of us. After dinner we'll watch the latest newsreel from the American Eighth Air Force . . ."

As they all listened to the commissioner's introduction, Helen's thoughts began to drift. She couldn't help thinking about Lillian's words, wondering about Harry's faithfulness. What would she do if she ever found out he was two-timing her and wouldn't be coming back? She realized she had so much invested in their future relationship, she'd be totally at a loss.

Toronto, Oct. 24 - Dec. 5, 1944 [excerpts]

My Darling Harry,

Well if it isn't Friday night again, and you're due for another letter honey, but very little has hap-pened since my last one.

However, I can tell you I'm all right and still thinking about you an <u>awful lot</u> – every spare minute, to be truthful.

Wednesday night I attended a Victory Loan dinner sponsored by the T.T.C. at the Savarin. There were about 250 there; six were represented from our office. After the dinner we were entertained by the usual speeches and newsreels. It was a very nice evening; I met a number of girls from H.O. and the other Divisions. Quite different from those parties held by the Steel Control in Ottawa!

You used to play at that Club, didn't you? I remember seeing the picture of your orchestra, which you have in your room.

I'm waiting until after this pay day, and will pay cash for it [i.e. the bond] *rather than have it deducted monthly – that's what I did last time.*

Velma and Vivie [Helen's younger sisters in Saskatchewan] *were "Miss Canadas" last week and sold $15 worth of War Savings Stamps* [worth about $200 today] *on a Saturday, which is fair for a small town like Melfort. I bet they looked cute as they almost look like twins. Jean (the oldest one) is sixteen today. A girl from home came up and spoke to me on the street car yesterday. I hardly recognized her as I haven't seen her for years.*

I'm told that there's about one fellow in a hundred who doesn't go on dates over there, and their girl friends or wives never hear about it. I would prefer to be told and if true, I'd do the same thing myself – I'm not kidding. It's up to both to play fair, don't you think? You know we didn't say anything about that before you went away – we just seemed to take it for granted. Well, I've never two-timed you, not once, and unless you've changed, I can't think you would either. Letters are proof anyway, and you've never let me down in that respect. Anyone could guess that with a glance at my file. Yes, you should almost be able to write a novel without effort after this.

Your Mother dropped in for a few minutes while I was working last night on her return from CFRB. I couldn't talk to her long though – she is looking well these days. Thursday is a busy day for them with the two broadcasts [one at CFRB and one at CBC]. *Don't you like the song "Someday I'll Meet You Again" or have you heard it?*

I hope you're keeping fit honey. I'm trying to, and am also learning to take waiting in my stride, but it isn't always easy, as you know.

Bye dearest.

All my love. Helen xxxxx

Bournemouth, Nov. 30, Dec. 19, 1944 [excerpts]

My Sweetheart Helen,

I just received your three letters of 3rd, 5th, and 7th today at long last; the post office is working over-time here what with so many parcels and extra letters so there's bound to be a little delay until after Christmas.

. . . . I suppose what you say about fellows going on dates is true, darling, but you must consider, before you class me with them, our different living conditions, which I think has a lot to do with it. How many of the chaps over here are living as comfortably as we are? I venture to say only the high ranking officers really. The only time I go out is when there is money involved [i.e. to play a dance job] *or very occasionally to a pub*

or show; you see we're here [in Bournemouth] *so seldom that we like to take full advantage of our good fortune – long may it last! I can't really blame fellows that have been kicking the streets for years before D-Day to break out once in a while, it's only human nature I guess.*

I don't wonder at you getting those silly notions into your head sometimes darling but I know you don't really believe them. It is awfully hard sometimes trying not to be impatient isn't it?

Well, sweetheart, I hope that little explanation clears your mind of any little doubts you may have had concerning myself. I want our love to last forever and am doing all in my power to see that it does and I never had any doubts whatever that you were too. . . .

All my love, Harry

Helen was comforted by Harry's assurance of his love and loyalty to her, which went a long way to bolster her to face the winter ahead. And she reflected that she was lucky to have picked the one fellow in one hundred who wouldn't cheat on her.

Harry's relatives and friends and, of course, Helen mailed many parcels to him, especially at Christmastime. They sent sweets such as chocolates, toffee, and fudge, as well as fruitcakes, tinned food, cigarettes, tobacco, crackers, cheese, peanut butter, soap, hand-knit socks, camera film, and, for the holiday season, liquor, if it was available. Harry also received packages from his old high school, Vaughan Collegiate, and Eaton's, where he had been working before he signed up. Some parcels were lost at sea, but surprisingly he received most of them, sometimes months after they were mailed. The deadline for Christmas boxes was approaching, and Helen was trying to get everything together.

She slumped into her chair exhausted, dropping her bags on the floor. She had just returned from the post office on St. Clair Avenue where they had told her the parcel she was sending to Harry was overweight. She'd have to take some things out and re-pack it, which she wasn't looking forward to.

The bottle of rum that Harry had asked for in his last letter was the tipping factor—it made up most of the weight.

Just then there was a knock at her door.

"It's the phone for you, Helen," said Mabel, her landlady's daughter. "I think it's Ida."

She went downstairs to answer it.

"Helen, do you have any room for some fruitcake in your box?" Ida asked.

"I'm afraid not. I have to take out something as it is because it's too heavy, but I'm not sure what at this point."

"All right, that's fine, I'll keep it for the next one. What are you sending him, anyway?"

"Oh, the usual, a tin of chicken, some crackers, peanut butter, the socks I just finished, the fudge I made at your place last week, and a bottle of rum for Victory Day, which he thinks will come before Christmas. That's what he asked for in his last letter."

"Well, according to the latest news, Victory Day might be a while yet; however, we can always hope."

"Oh, and by the way, he says he has lots of soup, hot chocolate, tins of spaghetti, and sardines, so don't send him any more for now," said Helen.

"All right. Glad he's got enough to keep him going for a while."

"Not that I have any room in this one, but did you find out if we can send newspapers over?"

"No, we can't. I called about it last week, and they're not allowed because of censorship."

Love in the Air

"All right. Bye for now."

Hanging up the phone, Helen went back upstairs to her lonely labour of love. As she packed up his parcel, she remembered how Harry would run his hand through her hair when he kissed her goodnight. He had such a loving touch. Her memories would have to sustain her until she could be near him once more.

Toronto, Oct. 20 - Nov. 24, 1944 [excerpts]

My Darling Harry,

Well, here it is Friday again - I've been working from 4:30 p.m. to 12:30 a.m. these last two nights as one of the men is sick. It has given me a chance to do a few things through the day—washing for instance and packing boxes. They are both on the way now—I had the second one all packed, decided it was rather heavy so took it down and had it weighed - 1 ¾ lbs. overweight so I began to unpack it. We do have our troubles too you see. You'll no doubt receive numerous parcels - better have a vacant corner in your room ready!

Have you been at home these last two weeks? Not exactly quiet in the southern sections according to reports. Well, I hope they stay away from the extreme coast anyway. There is certainly heavy fighting going on these days – with many reverses. It will be hard going once the cold weather comes.

Don't think I'm always asking – but listen – how about another snap of the two of you [i.e. Harry and Smitty] *with raincoats, hats and all? You have the film, so get Bill or somebody to take it the first sunny day.*

We were glad to know you received a couple of the parcels, you should have the one I sent about that time too. We noted the things you have a complete supply of – so will not include them again. Just don't hesitate to mention any little thing you like and know can be sent darling. Wouldn't mind getting packed in a box myself, if when I reached the destination I could pop out and look at you – oh shucks!

I enjoyed myself Wednesday, left here at 1:00 p.m. and went downtown. I was at a loss to know what to get Mother and Dad this year [i.e. for Christmas], *finally decided on a wine-coloured Morris chair, when I found out it could be sent for $1.00* [out to Saskatchewan.] *Eaton's pay the expenses to Kenora. Now Ray* [Helen's brother in the RCAF] *wants me to get them a present for him too.*

Don't I wish that was really a good night kiss of yours! Guess we'll just keep them for a little while yet – but oh! I'm always missing you honey.

Oct. 24, 1944 - It was announced the other day that there was a big fire in a Post Office in Montreal last Friday and a great number of Christmas parcels were burned. If you don't receive my first one, maybe that's what happened to it because I just mailed it on Thursday. I certainly hope you get it though.

Love, Helen

Mon. Nov. 20 – 30, 1944 [excerpts]

My Darling Helen –

Wow – what a day this has been. I was practically buried under an avalanche of parcels this morning when I went down for the mail.

I got three no less and everything was in perfect condition - even the bottle, thank heavens!

I think you need a well-deserved rest from packing boxes darling – we have enough food now to last for months. Smitty received one but is expecting more later.

You should have seen the smile on my face as I came out of the post office. I think the queue of P.O.'s [petty officers] *were a bit envious. I also received your letters of the 5*th, *7*th, *9*th *and 12*th. *Thanks for everything darling, I don't know what I'd do without you.*

Al just walked in with two big parcels of food! Our cupboard is just bulging with fruit cake and stuff. I received a rum and honey cake from George [Harry's uncle] *yesterday; it looks real nice. We'll be able to throw a big party here on Christmas if we can buy enough beer.*

I also got two dozen chocolate bars (Neilsons) from Vaughan Collegiate, very nice eh?

I almost forgot about the snaps; they're really swell. Oh darling, I love you so much.

Well, sweetheart, I'll have to close for now and get down to the sergeant's mess where there's never a liquor shortage. Bless 'em.

All my love angel – you sweet thing.

Hugs and Kisses. Harry.

14
Royal Bath Hotel

The stars are aglow
And tonight how their light sets me dreaming
My love, do you know
That your eyes are like stars brightly beaming
I bring you, and I sing you a moonlight serenade

"Moonlight Serenade," lyrics by Mitchell
Parish, music by Glenn Miller

Christmas decorations adorned the elegant King's Hall ball-room of the Royal Bath Hotel in Bournemouth; mistletoe hung in the doorways and ornaments sparkled atop the leaves of the potted palms surrounding the grand piano. The afternoon sun poured through the floor-to-ceiling windows, beyond which one could see the glistening waters of the English Channel. The hotel itself had not sustained any bomb damage thus far, but gaping holes were evident in the adjoining mansion belonging to the Russell-Cotes, the hotel owners.

For one day, the officers of the Royal Canadian Air Force and the Women's Auxiliary Air Force (WAAF) and their dates would try to forget about the war and enjoy a turkey lunch, followed by a dance.

The twelve members of the RCAF dance band went to the stage at the front of the ballroom, and unpacked their instruments and music stands. As they tuned up, the presiding sergeant came over to wish them a merry Christmas, then invited them to the bar for complimentary scotches and beer. Harry placed his tenor saxophone carefully down on the stand; he had just picked it up after having it repaired at Boosey's Music Shop in London, and he didn't want it to get damaged again.

The room started to fill up with happy revellers. As Harry and the others returned from the bar to start their set, they noticed three WAAFs fooling around with their instruments. One young woman was banging on the piano, while the other two had picked up the saxophones and were waving them in the air, pretending to blow, while laughing uproariously. The woman holding Harry's tenor hadn't realized how heavy it was and, when she saw the musicians approaching, accidentally dropped it.

"Is this your saxophone?" she asked sheepishly.

"Yes, unfortunately," Harry said, biting his lips, trying to contain himself. He looked at the instrument in dismay—one of the keys was broken.

"I'm so sorry, I just wanted to see if I could get a sound out of it," she apologized.

"I think this sax must be jinxed. I guess I'll send it back to get it fixed again, *for the third time*."

"But what will you play tonight?"

"Well, luckily I brought my clarinet, so you'll have to put up with that instead."

"Oh, I love the clarinet—Benny Goodman is my hero," she gushed. "See you guys later."

"What a bunch of dizzy dames," Harry said, thinking about how much more sensible Helen was, and wishing she were here instead of these intoxicated women.

"The blonde looked pretty good to me; maybe I'll ask her out tonight," Smitty said.

"At least she didn't damage your piano," Harry grumbled.

When Steve arrived, they started on a medley of jazzed-up Christmas carols, including "Jingle Bells" and "White Christmas." Harry whispered to Ossie that it seemed very odd to be playing those songs in a room overlooking a beach with tropical trees.

As the sun set on the channel and the light started to fade, they switched to dance tunes and people gradually went over to the floor.

After a while, Steve turned to face the crowd.

"We're sending out this next number in honour of Captain Glenn Miller, who you all know went missing over the channel on December 15, en route from Bedfordshire to Paris."[1]

As the band played Miller's signature tune, "Moonlight Serenade," the mood in the room went sombre, each one thinking about those who had been lost and loved ones back at home.

Dancers enjoying the music of the RCAF dance band

---

1   While travelling to entertain US troops in France in 1944, the plane Miller was on went down in the English Channel, and neither he nor the plane was ever found.

Bournemouth, Dec. 25, 1944

My Darling Helen,

Here I am sitting in front of the log fire again trying to organize my thoughts. We've been so busy since Wednesday sweetheart that I haven't had a minute to myself let alone time for writing. We played at the Airmen's Mess as usual this afternoon and had turkey afterwards. I've never seen so much kissing going on in my life everybody was running around with mistletoe on them, everybody seemed to have a good time.

Well darling, I took a job for tonight. Christmas is nothing when you can't be with those you love is it? Smitty is going out on a date so rather than sit here alone all night I thought I'd work. We'll be going to Gloucester tomorrow for a week of barrack life. I suppose I'll get plenty of rest there anyway.

Boy, am I full, we just finished some goose and Christmas pudding. I don't feel like working now, but I guess I'll have to.

You haven't told me what you bought yourself for Christmas from me, darling. I know it's not the nicest way to receive a gift but at least you get something you want.

Well darling, I must get dressed now as it's nearly seven.

I guess you heard about Glenn Miller being listed as missing.

Good-bye for now sweetheart and take care of yourself.

Joanne Culley

* * *

As the new year of 1945 began, the tide was turning in favour of the Allies. In early January, approximately ten million Russian soldiers started moving west from East Prussia, advancing on Berlin. By the end of the month, they were within fifty miles of the city. The Germans were being surrounded on all sides and, ever since D-Day the previous June, had been continually losing soldiers and armaments.

In Bournemouth, Harry and Smitty had to move when their landlady, Mrs. Hart, was ordered by her doctor to reduce her workload, as she had been preparing their meals, doing their laundry, and mending their uniforms. However, they found a spacious bed-sitting room at the Smiths', on Meyrick Park Road, in a district of spacious homes surrounded by a large park with bowling greens, tennis courts, and wooded paths.

In their new air force–issue overcoats, Harry and Smitty headed over to the Glue Pot Pub for a few pints. The full moon shone down on the snow that hung heavy on the tree branches as they walked through Meyrick Park. On their way over, they stopped to pick up Bill at his digs. As they entered the pub, the warm air and friendly chatter of the locals greeted them.

"What'll you have, fellows?" the barmaid asked them.

"Pints of Guinness all around," Bill ordered. He then turned to face Harry and Smitty. "Just got back from watching the latest newsreel. Looks pretty good, with the Russian army on the move."

"Yes, it does, but look at what happened in London last week—a rocket destroyed several buildings around the corner from where we usually stay. People are being killed there daily, according to the papers," Smitty said.

"Well, I think the end is in sight," said Harry. Smitty and Bill nodded, tentative yet hopeful.

After a moment's pause, Bill observed, "I hear some guys are thinking of staying here after the war; they think the work will be good."

"And some guys are already married to English gals—that would be an incentive to stay," added Smitty.

"Hard to know what's best, but I guess we'll cross that bridge when we come to it. By the way, how's your arrangement of 'I Cover the Waterfront' coming along? I think Steve needs it for the next dance," Bill asked Smitty.

"It's taking longer than I thought; I'm trying to work in a tenor solo for Harry here."

"Please don't, I have enough to practise as it is," Harry moaned.

"I heard the Ink Spots singing it on the radio last night—'I cover the waterfront, I'm watching the sea. Will the one I love, be coming back to me?'" Bill hammed it up.

"Well, my version will be less sappy and more jazzy."

"I can see you boys are happy. How's the beer?" the barmaid asked as she wiped the counter.

"Less watered down than up in Gloucester."

"Well, we do try to carry on as usual. Will you have another round?"

"Sure, it's a lot warmer in here than out there."

"They say it's the coldest winter in fifty years," she said, pulling the taps. "Where're you boys staying?"

"The Smiths', on the other side of Meyrick Park. Our pipes froze last night—the way it's going we'll have to melt the snow for water like we do in Canada!"

"Really? Well you won't catch me going over there like all those war brides. I just heard that over 40,000 British women are on their way to Canada—you boys sure have been busy."

"Well, I guess some of us are not totally focussed on the war effort," Bill said, giving her a wink. "But Canada's not so bad, although we do have a lot more snow than here, that's for sure. I think you'd like it there."

"No, thanks. It looks like the war won't be lasting too much longer and you can all go home to your sweethearts. What about this handsome fellow here?" she asked, looking at Harry. "Do you have a sweetie waiting for you, or would you like to stay here and keep me company?"

"Thanks for the offer, but I have a fiancée in Toronto," Harry said.

"This husband-to-be can hardly wait to get home!" Smitty added, nudging him.

"Let's drink to that!" They all raised their glasses in a cheer.

Bournemouth, Jan. 23, Feb. 4, 1945 [excerpts]

My Darling Helen,

I haven't received a letter from you since the one you wrote me on the 5th, isn't that terrible! They must be sending them over in rowboats or something. Everybody's is the same too.

As you've probably seen by the papers, they are getting a bit of snow over here now. There was quite a blizzard in London on Saturday afternoon and there's even a bit of snow down here but it's going to slush on the roads now. To make it worse there's a shortage of labour to deliver coal and a lot of old women are getting 6 shillings' worth of coal in a baby carriage, which is 14 lbs. Isn't that terrible! Our coal has run out but we still have lots of logs and coke.

Well honey, the only spectacular news around here is the Russians and the weather and the newspapers are filled with both. When we got up Friday morning we discovered the pipes in our toilet had frozen during the night and still are. Luckily they are the only taps that did freeze up so we can still wash and shave without having to melt the snow.

It's the coldest winter they've had here in fifty years and it's about 10°F out now, the ponds are frozen over and those who have skates are having a swell time, they say next month is going to be just as bad —brr. I hope our logs and coke hold out. We didn't have any trouble in getting up to Gloucester and back but the Glasgow trains were held up eleven hours on account of snow drifts. They've cut down electricity and even the electric clocks are running slow — isn't that funny? Also the gas at certain periods and it takes about six hours to cook a roast! So whether you have a coal or gas fire they defy you to keep warm; and you think you have troubles! But don't get the idea that I'm complaining or being morbid.

Well, darling, Smitty and I called on Bill this evening and went over to the Glue Pot for a couple of sociable beers. Al's working on a dance arrangement of "I Cover the Waterfront" and it takes up all his time. I'm reading a book on Wagner and his operas which is quite entertaining, so you see we manage to fill in our spare time all right.

I don't know what's in store for us next week but I hope we're not going anywhere until it gets warmer.

Well sweet, I honestly think this war is nearly finished; at the rate the Russians are advancing they should be in Berlin by the time you get this, but maybe I'm too optimistic; anyway it can happen so here's hoping.

The news looks so good these days, it can't last much longer. It looks as if it will go on until we take the last German town doesn't it?

Joanne Culley

Well, darling, I do write the same old stuff and I don't see how it can sound any different but I won't stop writing when that is all there is between us. A year and a half seems a long time to us now, but it doesn't count much in a life time does it? Well, sweet, I'll close for now but will write again in a couple of days.

Love, Harry

15
Snapshots

I never cared much for moonlit skies
I never wink back at fireflies
But now that the stars are in your eyes
I'm beginning to see the light

"I'm Beginning to See the Light," by Duke Ellington,
Don George, Johnny Hodges, and Harry James

Helen was off just one day a week, and this one found her
tidying up her room, doing laundry, washing her hair, and
ironing—she thought she might as well get it all done at once.

Her cousin Georgie was coming over after supper and Helen
was looking forward to it; they hadn't seen each other since
before Christmas. Helen laid out her fancy teacups and teapot
on the tray and put the kettle on the hot plate to boil.

Just then, she heard a knock.

"Hi, cuz, how are you doing tonight?" Georgie peeked her
head around the door.

"Come on in. I'm a little tired; I always am when I've just
come off nights. At least I'm not on that shift again for another
six weeks. I don't think I'll ever get used to it."

"That's what I thought—but at Inglis, as you know, we're on nights for two weeks and days for two weeks, so I think I'm more accustomed to it now. Oh, guess what? I got another letter from Bill!"

"That's good! I haven't had one from Harry for a while, but he did send me some snaps today."

"Bill said the band just got back from Stratford and London, where there was quite a bit of bombing. In my last letter, I'd asked him about his personality, and he was trying to describe himself, it was quite comical."

"What did he say?"

"Oh, that he was quiet, intelligent, and liked music—obviously—and that he had great plans for himself after the war."

"Well, that doesn't sound too bad to me—at least he's ambitious."

"I do like a fellow who enjoys a good time. Let me look at your band photos again; I'll see if I can pick him out. What a nice album."

"Ross and Elaine gave it to me for Christmas, and I just bought some white ink, so I've spent the last few days putting all of Harry's photos in order. Did I tell you Elaine had her baby on February 4?"

"No—how is she doing?"

"Fine. She just came home yesterday and the baby is sleeping pretty well. They're calling him David."

"That's nice. They must be very happy." Georgie brought the album closer. "Let me see. . . . Bill said he's beside Les, who plays the trumpet, so that must be him there," she said, pointing at the photo.

"Here's another one of just the dance band. Harry wrote on the back. Bill's on the right playing the upright bass. He looks very nice."

"Hmm. I thought he'd be a little taller. Well, we'll see what the situation is like when he returns."

"Have you seen your sergeant lately?"

"No, he was just on leave for thirty days, and I haven't had a letter or anything. Have you had any word from your brothers, Helen?"

"Yes, Jim wrote to say that he and Murray are being posted to a ship in the Atlantic, where it's been anything but quiet the last few days. And Ray's fixing planes near Gloucester."

As they continued poring over the photos, Helen thought about how it had been a year and a half since she'd seen Harry, and wondered how long it would be until the war was over.

"Oh, it's nine o'clock already. Let's listen to the news." Helen turned on the radio.

"The Western Front continues their advance and the long-awaited offensive is on," said the announcer. ". . . And here at home, in an upset result, General Andrew McNaughton has lost his bid for a seat in Grey-North County . . ."

RCAF dance band, Bill on right, Harry third from right

Toronto, Feb. 6 – Apr. 8, 1945, [excerpts]

Darling Harry,

I wasn't expecting all those snaps – thanks honey. They are all arranged already in the way I want them in my album. As I was looking at them, I was thinking of the fact that you had handled them; it's kind of a personal feeling. The one of you writing is cute, looks as if you're having a time propping it on your knee. How you ever carried kit bags with all other equipment, is a mystery. I'm glad you got those of Shakespeare's birthplace; isn't the garden path pretty? it looks it. Oh yes, I picked you out of that crowd at the Liverpool Hall, but you aren't in the other group of boys. They do look "well fed," all right.

Georgie came over on Sunday, she thought I had a grand collection of snaps and I think I have too. I wonder how a couple of those scenic ones would look enlarged. She had another letter from Bill; he was trying to describe himself and she said it was really funny. She was picking him out of each one of those pictures. She showed me those two snaps of Bill; one was taken with the members of the household where he stays and the other by himself. She liked them, but thought he was much taller. They all go for tall men. Maybe it was just the way he was standing, but he didn't look as tall as you, is he?

I walked down to the streetcar with her for the exercise.

Jim [Helen's brother] *mentioned in his letter that they were asking for volunteers for the Pacific, and he doubted if they would get out of it. I hope they don't* [have to go], *but we hear so many reports.*

The election brought a slight change yesterday eh? General Andrew McNaughton [commander of the Canadian army until 1943, when he became

Minister of Defence] *can't understand why he wasn't elected. He was running for Liberal member in the Grey North County and was defeated by Conservative Garfield Case. It seems he had to win the election in order to have a seat in Parliament, but the Public aren't for him now.*

The news from the front still continues to be good.

Frank Sinatra just sang "I'm Beginning to See the Light," have you heard it? He's on a new program now. I still prefer Bing though I think.

Well, sweetheart, guess I'll go to bed now; it's the limit how the time goes by when you're on my mind. It must be love – always yours.

Goodnight, xxx Helen

* * *

"I just found out that I'm getting Good Friday off tomorrow— you'd think they'd have given me more than a day's notice," grumbled Helen. "I didn't say anything, though, and I guess I'm not doing much anyway."

"Boy, planning ahead doesn't seem to be a strong point of the Motor Division, but the TTC in general is thinking about the future. Look at these plans."

Helen and Kay were browsing around the building drawings on display in the foyer on the seventh floor of Eaton's College Street.

"'The Rapid Transit Plans for Toronto.' My, that does sound grand," Helen commented.

"I wonder if they will ever be implemented?"

"Hard to imagine subways travelling underground through the city. Here's a photo of the Bloor Viaduct; it looks like they made provisions for tracks on the lower deck below the bridge when they built it back in 1918."

"Well, they need to do something to improve traffic flow; the jams last winter were really something."

"Look at this one, Kay—they're modelling the new Toronto subway on London's Underground. Harry will feel right at home when he returns."

"It all seems so fantastic."

"Yes, it does. We'd better go into the auditorium now. The commissioner is about to speak."

Toronto, March 29, 1945 [excerpt]

My Sweetheart Harry,

Look around – it's me again just to tell you that I'm fine and taking care of myself almost as well as you will be able to someday darling. I'm even going to be able to sleep in tomorrow. I was informed just before I left that I would have the holiday; they could have let me know sooner but not a word did I say. What will you be doing, I wonder. Playing an Easter Parade in the morning no doubt.

What are you hearing these days, darling? At present there is somewhat of a news blackout on the Rhine front, which they presume means a fast-moving advance. We all hope the climax is very close, - the great news that will be!

We saw "The Rapid Transit Plans for Toronto" last night at Eaton's College. This will really be "The Queen City" if they ever have them in operation. They plan to have natural parks and more beauty spots. They were showing many pictures of the London subways, the interior of the cars, etc. I could see the Palladium was situated on one of the corners. Then there were shots of the traffic jams here last winter; it seems unbelievable that they could have been that bad. The subway is to extend to Eglinton with a big station there.

Kay and I went down from work, and after that, had a lunch and went to "Shea's" to see "For Whom the Bell Tolls". It was a good picture.

Bing Crosby sang a couple of songs from "Star Spangled Rhythm" tonight. "Black Magic" was one. You remember when we went to that? "My Dreams are Getting Better" has been No. 1 on the Hit Parade for some weeks now.

Well honey, hope you're cheerful these days. We'll have so much to be thankful for when we can look at each other again. When I'm sleepy you just seem to weave into my thoughts. Nite nite. Always my love.

Helen. xxxx

* * *

"I'm glad you were able to come with me, Helen. This is so exciting!" Elaine said enthusiastically as they made their way to their seats in the CBC radio studio on Jarvis Street. "Ross is always working or away, so he's no company."

"I know how you feel; it gets very lonely sometimes for me also," Helen said as she sat down. "I haven't seen Harry's parents play live before—look, there's Howard Cable, the announcer, off to the side."

"Doesn't Ida's new gown look nice?"

"Yes, she bought it at Ira Berg's."

After a few minutes, Cable came to the microphone in the centre of the stage.

"Good evening, ladies and gentlemen in our live audience, as well as our listeners across the country. Welcome to Canadian Cavalcade. Our special guests tonight are the two-piano team of Claudette and Harry Culley, Toronto-born veterans of the variety stage and radio."

He paused while the audience clapped.

"Tonight, as a special treat, we will be interviewing this note-worthy duo before they entertain us. Would you both please come over to the microphone?" Ida and Harry Sr. appeared on stage to more applause. Cable continued, "Harry, I understand you do all of the arrangements for your performances."

"Yes, after the publisher sends us the music, I go through it and write out a second part."

"How often do you and your lovely wife practise?"

"Usually about two hours a day, one after the other, as we have only one piano at home." The audience laughed.

"Where did you find the score for your performance tonight?"

"When we were over in England before the war, we picked up a lot of music there that hadn't been released here yet."

"How would you describe your genre?"

"We call it 'Music for Moderns'—it hovers somewhere between symphonic music and the popular-hit parade melo-dies, songs like 'Kitten on the Keys,' 'Dizzy Fingers,' 'Marigold,' novelty pieces like that."

"And Claudette—that's your stage name, your real name is Ida—when did you start playing piano?"

"Oh, I've been playing by ear since I was three years old. I guess you'd say it's in my blood."

"I understand you both play popular hits on your other show."

"Yes, we play songs by Bing Crosby and Frank Sinatra on CFRB once a week."

"Well, we're certainly looking forward to your show tonight," Cable concluded. Then with a flourish of his arm he announced, "Please welcome Claudette and Harry Culley and their first piece 'Dizzy Fingers,' by Zez Confrey."

Elaine and Helen sat back to enjoy the piece, but before it ended they saw a script assistant rush over to Howard Cable with a piece of paper, and as he read it, his face darkened. After the applause, he stepped back to the microphone.

"We are interrupting this program to bring you the news that Franklin Delano Roosevelt, the thirty-second president of the United States, popularly known as FDR, has died at the Little White House in Warm Springs, Georgia. He became president in 1932 and led the US into the Second World War after the Japanese attack on Pearl Harbour in 1941. We now go to our reporters at the CBS station in New York City for more details. . . ."

At this announcement, the audience groaned as the live radio show ended.

Toronto, Apr. 12, 15 1945 [excerpts]

My Sweetheart Harry,

I have so many things on my lips to tell you that I have written often before, but if I could say them, they might sound different. Don't you think they would honey? I still haven't heard from you, and no one else seems to be receiving mail either. Eventually, something good must come of all this. I hope you are getting ours though.

Elaine phoned tonight and wanted me to go to see "Canadian Cavalcade" with her as your Mother and Dad were on. I felt somewhat tired, but wanted to see them, and was wishing you could have too. There was a short interview and they were asked how they practised, etc. She'll probably tell you about it. They played a "Concerto" and it sounded fine. The news came through about President Roosevelt at 5:00 p.m. Guess you wouldn't hear it until the morning. It seems tragic at this critical time, and in a short time he may have seen the end of it. He didn't look well in those pictures taken at the Yalta Conference, did he?[1]

Where did I leave off – oh, we came back to the house and after sitting awhile I felt more like lying down, so I did for a half hour in your room. I felt funny in there in the darkness when I thought of you darling. The others had gone when I got up, and we had a cup of tea. I didn't mind coming to work then.

Most of the scheduled programs have been can- celled the last three days. I've just been listening to the Trans Atlantic call; people from various parts of Great Britain were telling how the news of the President's passing affected them; maybe you heard it. It was all very sad. Even the people in those countries felt they knew him well. One of the reasons he was great was the way he overcame his physical handicap, that in itself required courage. I heard Duke Ellington's program last night, and he played some of his [Roosevelt's] favourite numbers on the piano.

Well, what do you think of things in general, darling – hopeful or otherwise? I'd like to know you so well someday that I'd always be able to read your thoughts – you might not like it though!

---

1   The Yalta Conference took place near Yalta in the Crimea from Febru- ary 4 to 11, 1945, where President of the United States Franklin Roo- sevelt, Prime Minister of the United Kingdom Winston Churchill, and Joseph Stalin, leader of the Soviet Union, met to discuss how Europe would be reorganized after the war.

Joanne Culley

I sent a parcel to you yesterday; made Georgian Date Squares along with those raisin cookies. Have you received the others yet?

Don't forget to vote on June 11th *twice* [i.e. once for the Member of Parliament and once for the Prime Minister.] *Tell me who you are voting for. I know very little about it, to tell you the truth. I hope we don't see the Liberals get in again though. I believe my Dad is still for the C.C.F., at least he used to be.*

Kent is supposed to be the most bombed area of Britain. They haven't had a bomb there in over three weeks, that's good, isn't it?

Well, I hope you're all right honey and think about me a few times. All my kisses are for you only and my love.

x x x x Helen

16
Heavy Costs of War

Roll out the barrel, we'll have a barrel of fun
Roll out the barrel, we've got the blues on the run
Zing boom tararrel, ring out a song of good cheer
Now's the time to roll the barrel, for the gang's all here

"Roll Out the Barrel," lyrics by Lew
Brown, music by J. Vejvoda

In early April 1945, the true horrors of the Nazi regime came to light, when the Allies liberated the Ohrdruf, Buchenwald, and Bergen-Belsen concentration camps as well as prisoner-of-war camps. The gruesome findings revealed the millions of inmates who had died or were deliberately killed and buried in mass graves. The Stalag Luft prisoner-of-war camps run by the German Luftwaffe held air force prisoners, many of whom were captured when their planes were shot down in enemy territory.

The war seemed to be coming to an end as the Allies overpowered the German armies near Bologna, Italy, on April 24 and when the Belorussians and Ukrainians surrounded Berlin on April 27. Still, the Germans refused to surrender.

* * *

On its way back from playing concerts in Birmingham, the RCAF band was transferring trains at Waterloo Station in London when it encountered an impromptu celebration on the main platform.

There was cheering and crying as some held up "Welcome Home" signs, while others waved Union Jacks. A group of gaunt-looking men in ragged RCAF uniforms wended their way through the crowds.

"What's going on?" Bill asked an onlooker.

"Some POWs have just returned from Germany. Are you boys in the RCAF band?"

"Yes, we're on our way back to Bournemouth."

"How about getting out your instruments?"

Bill checked his watch. "Sure, we've got fifteen minutes till our train leaves." He beckoned to Jonesy, who was on baggage detail, to push the heavily laden wagon over. The nearby band members unpacked their instruments and launched into "God Save the King" followed by "Roll Out the Barrel." Everyone joined in, singing and hugging the returnees.

Bill said they should get going or they would miss their train. As the band members took their seats, they realized the POWs were on the same coach.

"Where are you guys headed?" Smitty asked.

"Southampton. We're booked to go home on the Queen Mary, leaving for Halifax tomorrow," one of the stronger fellows said.

"That's good—you guys deserve special treatment."

Throughout the two-hour journey, the band members heard tales of the horrific experiences the men had endured. The lucky ones had worked hard on construction projects on meagre rations such as watery soup and black bread. The ones who hadn't survived had been shot while trying to escape, or had died of starvation. A couple had been on a forced march across Germany, before the Russians arrived, and had been rescued by the Allies.[1]

---

1   *A Time of Heroes: 1940/1950*, by Stephen Franklin

Upon reaching Bournemouth, Smitty and Harry walked home in silence, each pondering what he had just heard. Once again, they were reminded of the horrors of the war and felt guilty for complaining about their minor annoyances.

Harry was happy to find a letter from Helen waiting for him, and settled into the wing chair by the fire to read it.

Toronto, Easter Sunday, Apr. 1, 1945

My Only Darling Harry,

I've been sitting here for about five minutes just summing up the few things there are to tell you tonight. It's funny, all day I've been wishing you could see me and walk down the street with me, pretending in a way. Maybe I won't feel strange when you do. There was no letter yesterday, and I thought there would be. The holiday may have delayed the mail slightly.

As I told you, Friday was a holiday for me, so Kay and I went to the hospital to see a couple of boys, and Bill Stewart from the office is also in there. He's the one I mentioned, who was overseas for four years. He suddenly became paralyzed one night, from a heart condition and can't even feed himself; he'll be there indefinitely. I always feel so glad that I'm able to walk around when I leave a hospital. Kay came up with me on the Oakwood bus and we noticed that the show "Bowry to Broadway", or some such name, was on at the Oakwood so we went in. We got a few laughs, and felt better.

The reports of the combined offensives sound very good, then there's always a column of warning about the enemy going full strength in some sections. They'll hold out, but the leaders all say this is the last round.

It's late, late again honey, always after I write you I feel I'm back with you and there's just the two of us looking ahead, as we were meant to do.

My best love, Helen.

Bournemouth, Apr. 13, 25, 1945 [excerpts]

My own Darling Helen,

I have that awful empty feeling again tonight sweetheart for which you are the only remedy. Oh darling I miss you so much! It seems like a life time since I saw you last and it was for such a short time. I don't think either of us realized what a test this would be for us that night at the station. All I remember is that I was rather dazed and that I rushed off before my feelings got the better of me. I may add that rushing off didn't help much. Oh if I could only see you for even a minute or two, sweetheart, you'd know what your love does for me. I'll never leave you again sweetheart honest. Seems to me all I've been doing is talking about "I" so it's about time I changed the subject.

There was a regular home-coming for some Canadian RCAF POWs at Waterloo and they got on our coach. They had just been freed a week ago and had been flown here and were all excited. Our fellows got out their cameras and took pictures of them behind a big Nazi flag. One boy had an iron cross around his neck and nearly all of them had souvenirs of some kind. Their stories tally pretty well with what is in the papers.

Joanne Culley

Was terribly sorry to hear about Bill Stewart's condition, darling. Canada will be forever indebted to men like him. It makes me feel ashamed when I hear of cases like that really how little I am doing for the war effort – but I guess we can't all be engaging the enemy. It's rather hard to believe that the war is practically over after all these years and believe me the poorer people of London will certainly be relieved when it is. They're taking down most of the wire bunks in the tube stations where old women and kids have been sleeping for years. The trouble is they've been terribly slow in putting up these boxes they call prefabricated houses due to the labour shortage so there's bound to be a muddle for several months after V-Day.

Well, sweetheart, Smitty has just come in and we are making some sandwiches for our 12 hr. trip tomorrow to South Wales so will say good-bye for now dearest.

My eternal love angel. Harry

* * *

Smitty and Harry were walking home through Meyrick Park after seeing the movie *A Song to Remember* at the Regent Theatre in downtown Bournemouth.

"I enjoyed the film, but I wonder, how closely did it depict the life of Chopin?" Smitty asked.

"Probably quite a sentimental, romantic version—Merle Oberon as George Sand was a bit over the top, in my opinion."

"I agree, but I loved the piano playing, even if the stars didn't actually do it themselves."

"Yes, it's amazing how they can make it look so real. I liked the part when Chopin and Liszt shook hands while playing the

Love in the Air

Nocturne together, one with his right hand and the other with his left."

"That was quite a stunt. Do your parents include tricks like that with their two-pianos, four-hands routine?"

"No, they're pretty serious when they're playing, and besides, their grands are end to end, so it wouldn't be physically possible," Harry said.

"Do they still perform regularly?"

"Yes, on the radio and stage. Their work really picked up after they got back from England at the beginning of the war. They were here in the British Isles for about two years, including time in South Africa. They went back home when it looked like war was brewing. Who would've ever imagined that it would go on for six years?"

"Well, it looks like it's nearly at the end, what with Hitler gone and Berlin surrendered, it seems to be all over but the shouting," Smitty commented.

"I guess we can expect the big news any day now."

A gentle breeze wafted through the elm trees as they left the park, crossing under the stone bridge and making their way up their street.

"Do you hear that? It sounds like a piano. Someone's playing 'Tenderly'—that's my mother's favourite song," said Harry.

They walked up the driveway in order to listen better.

All of a sudden, the music stopped, a door flung open, and a distinguished, grey-haired gentleman demanded to know what they were doing.

Smitty was the braver one. "We heard the amazing piano playing and wanted to get nearer," he ventured.

The gentleman's face softened. "Well, come on in and you can hear me playing it in the same room."

Bournemouth, Apr. 28, 1945

My Darling Helen,

Received your two letters of 15th and 19th and am so glad mine are reaching you at last. It is provoking to think that they can't keep up a regular service isn't it? I mentioned it to the other Toronto boys and their wives were complaining about it too.

Smitty and I had a funny experience the other night coming home from a show. We were walking past a terrific house when I happened to hear a piano so I stopped for a minute and it sounded pretty good. So Smitty said "Let's walk up the drive where we can hear it better" so we did. No sooner had we got where we could hear but he [the pianist] *stopped and came out and asked what we were doing there. I nearly died, but he immediately invited us in for a beer. He and his wife made us feel at home in no time and I asked him to play a few things for us. One of them was "Marigold."[2] Mother and Dad play it. He was playing on a Steinway grand which was in a room off the living room but he had another upright piano in the living room. He knows Carroll Gibbons quite well and even plays like him.[3] He said he recognized Mother when I showed him a picture of the two of them. So he invited the two of us back next week for a "jam session"!! How's that for a novel way of meeting the right people?*

---

2   "Marigold" was a popular composition by Billy Mayerl, an English composer and pianist.

3   Carroll Gibbons was an American pianist and bandleader who moved to England in 1924 and became well-known by playing piano at the Savoy Hotel in London. He also helped to found the Savoy Orpheans, a jazz group, and the New Mayfair Dance Orchestra.

I'll close for now dearest. Another Saturday night is here and no place to go. Wish I had a job.

All my love darling, always and always. Harry xxxxxxxx

P.S. The International Ballet is here next week so I'll be down to see them – you didn't like Prince Igor eh?

P.P.S. Bill is about the same height as I am only heavier.

P.P.P.S. I love you.

|7
Victory in Europe Day

Land of hope and glory, mother of the free
How shall we extol thee, who are born of thee
Wider still and wider shall thy bounds be set
God, who made thee mighty, make thee mightier yet

"Land of Hope and Glory," lyrics by A. C.
Benson, music by Edward Elgar

The sun streamed in through the bay window as Smitty opened one eye and reached over to the radio to turn on the news.

"Prime Minister Churchill is expected to make the declaration of peace later today, May 8, 1945," said the BBC announcer. "Stay tuned for the latest developments."

"Harry, wake up, I think today's the day!" Smitty shook him. "Listen."

". . . The Canadian army in Holland is being repatriated after a successful liberation of that country," continued the announcer.

"Let's go downtown and see what's doing."

They dressed hurriedly and headed out. As they walked through the square, they could see the shop owners draping

Union Jacks over the doors and putting up bunting on the windows.

"Has Steve given any orders about our duties for Victory in Europe Day?" Harry asked.

"Not yet, although it's likely he'll have a parade cooked up."

"Now that you're a corporal and higher than us lowly privates, we'll all look to you for the inside scoop," Harry kidded Smitty, who had just received a promotion.

"Will you leave off already? It's bad enough the ribbing I'm getting from the other guys, please don't you start. I really don't feel any different, but I guess I'll get a little more pay."

They headed over to the Norfolk Hotel, across from the *Bournemouth Daily Echo* office.

"If there's anywhere to be in Bournemouth, this is probably it," Harry said.

British, Canadian, and American service personnel and civilians crowded the ballroom, talking, drinking, and smoking together in anticipation of the joyous news. The hotel staff was hooking up loudspeakers to a radio in front. At precisely 3 p.m. the unmistakable voice of Prime Minister Winston Churchill boomed through the room.

"Hostilities will end officially at one minute after midnight tonight. We may allow ourselves a brief period of rejoicing. . . ."

At that, everyone cheered.

". . . This is your victory. Victory in the cause of freedom. In all our long history, we have never seen a greater day than this. Everyone, man or woman, has done their bit. None have flinched. . . . God bless you all."

Someone started singing "Land of Hope and Glory" and they all joined in, laughing and crying at the same time.

"Land of Hope and Glory, Mother of the Free, . . . Thou hast reigned victorious, thou has smiled at fate. . . . Lo, our lips are thankful, lo, our hearts are high!"

Slowly the band members left the hotel and walked back through the square and up to the Atherstone Hotel, where Les and Bill were boarding.

"What better time to break out my latest parcel from home," Les announced as they entered the tiny room.

He unpacked tins of Spam, cheese, cookies, and chocolate bars and offered them around.

Bill got out some rum and Coke and they held up their glasses in a toast.

"To the end of this long, bloody war."

As Harry raised his glass, all he could think about was how soon he could take Helen in his arms and kiss her all night long.

> *Bournemouth, Tues., May 8, 1945 VE Day, 12 midnight*[excerpt]
>
> *My Sweetheart Helen,*
>
> *This is the day we've all been waiting for. . . . It's pretty hard to realize now that the war is over. When you consider that three years of your life have been moulded around wartime conditions and now all that is at an end. The news will seem pretty tame now won't it?*
>
> *. . . One of the boys who just received a parcel invited us over to his hotel to have a feed. . . .Well, after finishing off 5 tins of Spam I spent most of the afternoon lying in bed while the rest of them got to work on rum and cokes. I only had one drink believe it or not. I've never seen Smitty get so flushed in the face as he was this afternoon; he was almost purple!*
>
> *The landlady invited the ones who could walk down for tea and after that we all went over to the Bowling Green to see the boys who were playing. I didn't stay long as it was unbearably close and*

sultry all night with low rain clouds, just like it gets in Toronto in the middle of summer. I walked over to the Pavilion to see the fountain with a POW who was with us and spent a few minutes looking at the constant changing of colours and patterns. It's really pretty to watch, but we soon got tired of that and went down to the beach and sat down to get cooled off. There was a big bonfire going on the sand with hundreds of people around it singing old songs; they were using deck chairs as fire wood. There was another fire going up in the park.

It was getting late and my feet were getting awfully tired so I decided to head home, and was it dark! The only light to be seen was at the Norfolk Hotel and the people flocked around it like moths. They had floodlights on it and the violinist from the orchestra was playing on the balcony for the crowds. It sure was a feast for the eyes to see all those lights.

Well sweetheart space is running short so will close for now. I love you darling.

All my love Harry xxxxxx

Toronto, May 7, 1945 [excerpt]

My Only Sweetheart Harry,

What a day honey! I'm still going around in a daze really. At present it is 9:40 p.m. and I am writing at your dining room table, after having seen the show "A Song to Remember" at Shea's. I jumped out of bed at ten when I overheard the news on the radio in the next room [of the official surrender.]

She [her landlady] *said it was true, and I walked back and forth to compose myself or try to. It just happened I had the day off as I worked yesterday instead, wasn't that nice. As I didn't get a call in a half hour I phoned your Mother and she hadn't even heard it. Your Dad was still in bed . . . Then I said I'd come down about one. To add to this, I received your letter of April 28th. It all made me feel the bridge wasn't so far between us, and your P.P.P.S. on the bottom was so sweet. Oh darling! the thoughts of seeing you thrill me even though I know it will be three to six months. Even the air is different, no kidding.*

. . . We were downtown in the mob and we sat on the steps at the City Hall until after three, to see if the official announcement would come, but apparently it has been postponed until tomorrow. At least King George and the other leaders are speaking then. We walked back and saw lots of gay people really doing the town and a couple of accidents, but they had calmed down a bit tonight.

I told your parents about you meeting that pianist. Did you enjoy your second visit? That was swell. The news reports say the Canadian service men really did it up in London. Guess you won't be there, will you? We just looked out the window and the fireworks are going off.

My parents heard your parents' program on Canadian Cavalcade. I am excited darling. What will it be like when you come? All day tomorrow those thoughts will run through my mind. Here's to us. I love you dear.

Always yours. Helen

18
Looking to the Future

Well, what do you know, he smiled at me in my dreams
last night
My dreams are getting better all the time
And, what do you know, he smiled at me in a different
light
My dreams are getting better all the time

"My Dreams Are Getting Better All the Time,"
lyrics by Manny Curtis, music by Vic Mizzy

A few days after VE Day, Helen went over to her cousins' apartment to celebrate.

"I still can't believe it's finally over," said Georgie as she brought in the teapot and cookies.

"Yes, it's been going on so long, I was worried it was going to last forever," Helen sighed as she sunk into the easy chair.

"It's great to see the flags flying and all the streamers in the shops."

"I hung out two flags from my window to show that I'm doubly happy that it's ended. It's a good thing the celebration didn't turn into a riot here like it did in Halifax. They say the damage was close to five million dollars. The papers blame the naval authorities. The sailors always were unpopular; they'll have a terrible time now. I'm glad my brothers Jim and Murray weren't there," Helen said, sipping her Earl Grey.

"Murray, at any rate, was always out for a good time—I think Glady had her eye on him," Georgie replied, smiling.

"Too bad they're cousins. Yeah, I worry about them both, being their older sister. I hope they don't have to go to the Pacific now."

"Have you finished your tea yet? Let me read your tea leaves. . . . Hmmmm . . ." Georgie looked intently at the bottom of Helen's flowered china cup. "You will be seeing a tall, dark, handsome man sometime in the next few months." She looked up mischievously. "I wonder who that could be?"

Helen smiled, embarrassed. "I'm finding myself getting quite impatient for Harry to come home, but I know it will be quite a while. Oh, did I tell you that in the last letter he said that Bill is about 5'11", the same height as Harry is?"

"That'll do. He hasn't written me since April, though, but a certain sergeant has been sending me quite a few love letters. We'll have to see who gets home first!" Georgie laughed.

"I was reading in the paper today that it was almost like VE Day all over again at Union Station the other night. One fellow was greeted by his wife, his eight sisters, and his mother, and what a grand-looking group they were!"

Just then Georgie's sisters, Billie, Glady, and Donny, came in from shopping and squealed at the sight of Helen.

"Oh, cuz, we're so happy for you—finally it's over and your sweetie can come home."

"Yes, I can hardly wait," Helen said, and thought to herself that she could hardly wait to feel his loving arms wrapped around her, safe in the knowledge that he wouldn't be leaving her again.

Toronto May 16, 1945

Darling Harry,

I went over to Georgie's last night and came home about eleven. As I put my hand on the banister, on the way upstairs, there your two letters were, dated 7th and 8th. I had been waiting to hear how you spent the big days . . . At the fountain and the beach – I would like to have been with you. No wonder the people gazed at the floodlights, after seeing darkness for so long. . .

World affairs are far from being settled yet. The countries have so many differences and the big factor seems to be Russia. It is to be hoped the next big meeting will clear up matters quietly, or the result might not be pleasant.

Georgie had one letter from Bill the latter part of April. She hears from her Sergeant Murray very often and is becoming more interested in him. She expects he'll be home in July, as he's been over three years. Anyway we agreed we'd have a night out – the four of us, either with Bill or Murray, whoever it happened to be. Is that all right by you honey? As for the date, that will be left open. Oh! he sent her some German money and she gave me some.

I don't know what I'll say to you, but the words will come straight from my heart. Goodnight dear, all my love Helen xxxxx

* * *

With the military men gradually returning from the war, working women in Canada realized that a number of them would have to give up their jobs. Many workplaces had policies that servicemen had first priority, with women being let go. And there were also rules that stated when a woman married, she had to leave her position.

"You writing Harry?" Kay asked Helen as she entered the lunchroom at the TTC.

"Yes, I thought I'd grab a spare moment to let him know that I'm thinking about him."

"I guess the men will all be heading home soon—they've been letting the women go here one by one, starting with the drivers and clerks. I've noticed quite a bit of tension around. It's just you, me, and Connie left. I wonder when we're next."

"Well, not many of the men know shorthand or typing, so we should be good for a while."

"Let's hope so. I've got my mother to take care of—I don't know what I'll do if I'm laid off," Kay said. "Do you know when Harry will be back?"

"No, I think it will be some time yet. I read in the paper yesterday that there are 200,000 men and women to come back. At the rate of 25,000 a month, it could take eight months for everyone to come home, considering the amount of space available on the ships," replied Helen.

"Is there some kind of point system?"

"Yes, I believe each soldier is assessed according to his length of service, type of duty, and other factors. For instance, the POWs are a higher priority than the band members."

"Do you know what Harry's number is?"

"I think he said eighty-four in one of his letters, but I'm not sure what that means compared to the others."

"Oh well, let's hope it's not too far off."

Toronto May 18, 1945

Dear Harry,

Today I'm writing you at noon hour, as it is pay day and nearly everyone has gone to the bank, but

I don't always need to cash mine the first day I get it!

I made a few snappy remarks [at work] *this morning, and the chief clerk said he guessed the mail had been held up again. That wasn't called for, but I laughed it off. Quite a number of fellows are coming back to their jobs here, as drivers, and clerks. Three airmen were in this morning. Then the two new clerks we have are back from overseas. There are only three of us girls left, so I hope they decide they still need stenos, as I'd rather stay here than be transferred to another Division or Head Office, as it might mean a decrease in salary.*

Honey, I can't say this all in one breath without asking what you're doing and all that. I know if you are informed of anything new, you will tell me quickly [i.e. when he will be coming back]. *Don't keep it as a surprise please. This is one time when I want to know much beforehand. They tell me the months will go quickly, but my own little idea is that they will drag, but maybe not too much, what say darling? It's hard not to talk about it a little bit, as it seems foremost in everyone's thoughts. So long sweetheart, time's up. If I were to hear your voice now I'd feel all funny, I know it.*

Yours with love. Helen

Love in the Air

|9
On the Move Again

I'll be seeing you
In all the old familiar places
That this heart of mine embraces
All day and through

"I'll Be Seeing You," lyrics by Irving
Kahal, music by Sammy Fain

Over the three years they'd been in the RCAF, Smitty and Harry
had become close friends, almost like brothers, tolerating each
other's foibles with respect and good humour.

Once again the pair found themselves moving into a new
room together after being evicted from the Meyrick Park
mansion where they were boarding. Their landlady's London
friends were about to arrive to spend their summer vacation at
the Bournemouth beach.

"From riches to rags in one jump," Harry moaned as they
lugged their bags up four flights of stairs to the tiny room.

"I wonder how many more times we'll have to move before
we finally go home," Smitty mused somewhat ruefully.

"Just think, I carried everything off the boat all at once, including my clarinet, and now it takes four trips. We'll have to get a taxi tomorrow to bring the rest of it."

"And we'll have to throw out a lot of stuff before we get on that ship," Smitty commented, looking down at Harry's box. "You know, you could get rid of those letters."

Harry glared at him, so Smitty knew better than to pursue that line of thought.

"Quite the Bohemian atmosphere," Smitty observed as they dropped their kit bags on the floor.

"I guess it isn't too bad for fifteen shillings a week, but I hope the roof doesn't leak," Harry said, moving over to the turreted window. "Look—you can see the RCAF headquarters from here."

"Yes, being on Christchurch Road has its advantages. We're quite close to everything—the rehearsal hall, the town hall, the Pavilion. Well, we'd better get down to the food office to get our ration coupons if we're going to have anything to eat for supper."

Bournemouth, June 3, 7, 1945 [excerpts]

Dearest Helen,

Yes, sweetheart, we've got a room, we looked at it a couple of weeks ago but held out hoping for something better, but something better didn't turn up. It has one good point anyway – we can see Bath Hill Court from the window (that's RCAF HQs) and it's about five minutes from where we rehearse. Oh yes another good point – it faces south and is light and airy! I hope there aren't any bats in our belfry!

I have to get rid of a lot of stuff before I go home. No darling, I didn't tear up your letters. I have every one of them since Halifax. Smitty thinks

I'm crazy – maybe I am – about you. I did away with a lot of Christmas cards from two Christmases ago though there's no room in the place for anything. He says I have a mania for collecting things.

Smitty and I just came back from the food office where we registered our change of address. What a mob of women were there! Fortunately a clerk took pity on us and allowed us to break the queue. I felt like a heel for doing it, but we'd be silly not to. I sure feel sorry for English housewives with all the red tape aimed directly at them. We had to change our grocer, butcher, and milk man because you have to deal where they tell you, you know, and besides, the old ones were too far away anyway. We can now get ½ pt. of milk each morning and a shilling's worth of meat a week apiece which is double the meat ration civilians get. They say things will be better next autumn though. There are more cars on the road now that the basic ration is 1 gallon a week. I think we'll like our new room honey as the people who own it seem very nice and seem willing to cooperate. We were invited downstairs last night and the husband played the piano for us.

We filled out a form this afternoon; they want to know our preference as to service [after the war], whether occupational in Germany, the Far East or Canada. It took me a long time (a split second) to make up my mind but I said I preferred service in Canada to the rest and a discharge thrown in. Only one guy volunteered for service in the Far East and that's because his Mother-in-law is waiting for him with a battle axe!

Darling, as soon as I hear even the slightest rumour of our going home I'll write and let you know. My number is 84 but I don't think we'll be sent home individually. I'll wire you as soon as I find out anything definite. What's your phone number darling? I might even phone you. Wouldn't you be surprised? Yes sweetheart the time does drag terribly and always has. How else could it be away from you?

I'm always thinking of you sweetheart and always shall.

All my love darling,

Harry xxxxxx

* * *

The RCAF No. 3 Personnel Reception Centre Band was in London for several days of parades and concerts in July 1945 to celebrate Canada's involvement in the war and the country's Dominion Day (now known as Canada Day). The mood in the city was much more festive and relaxed than it had been during the dark days of the war.

The band led a parade of army, navy, and air force personnel on Monday, July 2, 1945, starting from the Wellington Barracks and passing by the Duke of York Steps, where the Honourable Vincent Massey, Canadian High Commissioner, took the salute.[1] They finished at Westminster Abbey, where there were Protestant services, and Westminster Cathedral, where there were Catholic services. Newsreels of the parade were shown around the world.

---

1   Vincent Massey was High Commissioner to Great Britain for Canada, posted at Canada House. He later served as Governor General of Canada from 1952 to 1959.

Joanne Culley

*RCAF No. 3 Personnel Reception Centre Band on parade
with Honourable Vincent Massey on platform at right*

The highlight of their visit was a large massed-band concert near the RCAF Overseas Headquarters at Lincoln's Inn Fields, the largest public square in London, on July 3, 1945, conducted by Martin Boundy, the head music director of the RCAF. Photographs of this concert appeared in the *Canada News Weekly* and later in books about the war.

Located at 20 Lincoln's Inn Fields, the RCAF headquarters provided support to the approximately 85,000 Canadians who were part of forty-eight squadrons during the Second World War.

Several band members boarded the double-decker bus from where they were staying at the Knights of Columbus on their way to the concert.

"Look, guys, we can finally see where we're going! They've taken the netting off the windows," Harry said.

"And we don't have to worry about a stray V-2 coming our way," Bill added.

"Things sure are looking up."

"Well, I hope Boundy isn't too hard on us," said Smitty.

Harry chuckled. "I'm sure it will be cacophony—all three bands thrown in together."

"I hope it goes all right, with all the photographers, reporters, and cameramen running around."

"I'd like to see the newsreel of us at the Mall yesterday. The cameraman had quite a time keeping his balance on top of the Bentley as we marched by."

"Likely the shots will be wobbly."

As they entered the square, they were astounded.

"There must be 3,000 people here. Can you believe it?"

"I guess the Londoners are so weary from the war that they'll listen to anything!"

RCAF massed band in Lincoln's Inn Fields, London, Harry Culley is fourth from right in second row playing clarinet

Bournemouth July 5, 1945

My Sweetheart Helen,

Well, I suppose you will want to know all about what we did in London eh? They managed to keep us very busy on Mon., Tues. and Wed. Our band took the parade from Wellington Barracks

Trafalgar Square & Cenotaph on Whitehall to Westminster Abbey. They took movies of the parade so you might see some of the band in the newsreels. We played at the opening of the Lord Tweedsmuir Officer's Club in Regent's Park yesterday and while I was playing billiards in the games room a photographer from Canada News came in and took a picture of me making a shot![2] Needless to say I missed it and the ball was right over the pocket too. We had a swell supper just before we left with ice cream and fruit. I think it used to be his home in London, the S.A. [Salvation Army] *are supervising it.*

Monday afternoon after the parade they held a massed band rehearsal by the three bands, about 140 men I guess, so by the time 6 o'clock came around I was pretty tired. I went around the corner for a beer with Bill. Tues. morning we had another rehearsal and then played in Lincoln's Inn Fields for a noon hour concert under the trees. Gosh it was warm in London and so close especially in the tubes.

They've taken the netting off the windows of the buses & tubes so you can see what station you're pulling into now without peering through a hole.

Well, sweet, two months since the peace was declared and still no word about when we're going home! I suppose they won't give us much warning when they finally make up their minds to send us but I'd like to have some idea that's all.

---

2   John Buchan, 1st Baron Tweedsmuir, was a Scottish novelist, lawyer, and politician who was Governor General of Canada from 1935 to 1940.

A few officers in the transient band volunteered for Burma and are going home right away so that leaves a job for me for three nights a week at the Westover [in Bournemouth]. *It was originally an ice rink but was taken over by the RCAF and used as a dance hall. It's not far from here and finishes at 11, so it will be better than jobbing all over the country side.*

So now we're going to have a tin of sardines and go to bed; thrilling isn't it? We're getting used to the room now. We didn't get back from London last night until after 11 and luckily we're only a few minutes' walk from the station. One of the boys lives farther out than we used to and as the buses stop running at nine he didn't get home until after one as he was on baggage detail too.

Well, sweetheart, I'll close for this time as it's getting late and we have to get up at eight. All my love angel. I'm always thinking of you.

Harry xxxxxx

Toronto, July 28, 1945 [excerpts]

Darling Harry,

. . . I wasn't able to see the newsreel at the Tivoli, but I phoned Famous Players, then Paramount and was informed it would be at the Bloor next week, so I hope to see it. Your mother said I might jump out of my seat [i.e. if she saw Harry in it].

Toronto, Aug.1, 1945 We went to see the newsreel Monday evening, and I just caught a glimpse of

*you. I was so busy looking you know how it is.
I wish they hadn't turned it so fast. They only
showed it once, as the feature was long. I came
directly home as I was quite tired.*

*I hope you're able to get that magazine. Is it a
good picture of you?*

Love, Helen

20
The Atom Bomb and V-J Day

Over hill, over dale, we will hit the dusty trail
As the caissons go rolling along
Up and down, in and out, countermarch and right about
And our caissons go rolling along

"The Caisson Song," by Edmund L. Gruber,
William Bryden, and Robert Danford

Even though the war in Europe had ended in May 1945, the war in the Pacific continued, led by the United States, which had declared war on Japan the day after Japan bombed the American naval base at Pearl Harbor, Hawaii, on December 7, 1941, thus joining the other Allied Nations in the Second World War. By April 1942, Japan was occupying the Philippines, Indochina, and Singapore. American troops dominated the fighting in the Pacific, helping to avert further expansion of the imperialist Japanese empire.

The war in the Pacific culminated when the United States dropped two atomic bombs on Japan at Hiroshima on August 6, 1945, and at Nagasaki on August 9, 1945, killing approximately 200,000 people.

Bournemouth, Aug. 9, 13, 1945 [excerpts]

Dearest Helen,

The papers are full of the new invention, the atom bomb and the damage it did to the city of Hiroshima. I can't see any argument to justify using it to kill 100,000 civilians, can you? It's just one step further to the end of civilization as we know it as far as I can see. But I hope I'm wrong. I'd like a few years of peace with you darling before we all get blown off the earth!

Well darling, I suppose it's just a matter of hours until there will be peace on earth again for the first time in eight years. It doesn't seem natural to know that there isn't a fight going on in some part of the world. I sure hope that speeds up our return home. . .

Love, Harry

With the devastation caused by the atomic bombs, the war in Japan ended on August 15, 1945, commonly referred to as Victory over Japan Day, or V-J Day. The official signing of the formal surrender document took place on September 2, 1945, in Tokyo Bay, Japan, aboard the ship the USS *Missouri.*

Harry had been in bed for just an hour in the early morning on August 15, 1945, when he heard some kids hollering and blowing noisemakers down below his room on Christchurch Road. He turned on the lamp and peered at the clock—12:30 a.m. Harry thought it was strange that kids would be out so late, then he realized—the war in Japan and all of the Second World War were finally over.

Smitty rushed in and told him that the good news was broadcast at midnight.

"What an ungodly hour—but I guess we better get over to the square," Harry said, pulling on his pants.

Once outside, they heard an American dance band marching down the street playing "The Caisson Song."[1]

Everyone started singing: "Over hill, over dale, we will hit the dusty trail as the caissons go rolling along."

"The unofficial song of the US Army," Smitty shouted over the din.

Another American band was perched on the roof of the bus depot, playing for the crowds gathering around a huge bonfire in the square. For the second time in three months, the city was going wild with celebrations.

Bournemouth, Aug. 15, 1945 VJ Day 2 p.m.

Dearest Helen,

The war is over at last! It seems almost unbelievable to me that factories won't be making shells and guns any more and that men will all be going home at last instead of setting out for battle fronts all over the world.

Smitty came in and just then an American dance band came marching down the street playing "The Caissons go Rolling Along", so sleep was out of the question and I got up and we went down to the Square. There must have been at least a thousand people there around a big bon fire built in the middle and the dance band was up on the roof of a bus station going to it and giving out with plenty of jazz. It was really an American celebration all the way. They had conga lines all over the place and a baton twirler like I've never seen before. We hung around until about 2 a.m. and then came home to bed.

---

1   A caisson is a chest to hold ammunition.

We had to report at 10 a.m. this morning but there was nothing for us to do except that the dance band is playing at the Mess Hall (Winter Garden) to-night. I suppose we'll be doing a big parade on Sunday.

We just live around the corner from where the WAAF is billeted and they have the misfortune (?) to have a pub right in the same hotel. There's a couple of them drunk as lords carrying Union Jacks and shaking hands with everybody on the street saying "We beat them again!" I guess you wonder why I'm not out doing the same? Well, I just received your letter of 7th and 9th[2] this morning and I couldn't feel any happier if I tried. Darling, the only music and words I want to hear when I get off the train is your voice speaking my name. I've dreamed of it so often it almost seems real sometimes sweet. I know we must think of each other often at the same time darling because I always seem to have you in my mind at all times. Yes, angel, our time will come soon but we mustn't get too anxious. Look who's talking!

There's no one more anxious to use my uniform for a door mat than I am. My shirts were all in ribbons almost and Mrs. Forster [his landlady] *has just done a fine job of patching them. The uniform is really a wreck too and is every colour except blue. Do I worry? Not when I'm making $50 a week.*

You can close your eyes when I kiss you sweetheart but you won't have to open them to make

2 Helen's letters from August 7 and 9, 1945 appear in Chapter 21.

Joanne Culley

sure I'm still there. I'll be there all right, just as close as you want me.

Well, sweetheart, I've spent all afternoon with you again and now it's time to clean up and get tea. I hope everybody gets too drunk to dance any later than 12 tonight because if they don't we'll all have to play until 1 or 2.

All my love angel, Harry

Amidst the jubilation of victory were the reminders of the horrible and tragic consequences of the war. The Queen Victoria Hospital at East Grimstead, south of London, became world renowned for its treatment of severely burned war victims, with innovative methods of reconstructive plastic surgery developed by Dr. Archibald McIndoe. Patients were Allied air force personnel burned while on duty as air crew. Plastic surgery on burn victims was performed there from July 1944 on. No mirrors were allowed in the hospital, and the employees and citizens in the nearby towns were encouraged to treat the patients as normally as possible to aid in their psychological recovery.

A new Royal Canadian Air Force wing built by the Royal Canadian Engineers was officially opened at the hospital on September 5, 1945.

The RCAF No. 3 Personnel Reception Centre Band had just marched three miles from the town of East Grimstead to the hospital. Lining up on the grounds of the facility, they were waiting for the ceremonies to begin.

"That was one of the longer parades we've done. All the way from town out into the countryside," moaned Bill.

"Did you know they also want us to play a dance here tonight?" asked Harry.

"But we didn't bring the dance music library," said Smitty. "Or the instruments."

"Jim has gone back for the instruments, but as for the music, we'll have to wing it."

"I guess that's why they call us the air force band." They all groaned at that one.

"Lots of bigwigs here—Frederic Hudd, Acting High Commissioner for Canada, Air Marshal Johnson . . ."

"Look, there's the chief surgeon, Dr. McIndoe."

The band members watched as the nurses in their white starched caps and uniforms wheeled out the patients who were able to sit up, their heads swathed in bandages, some missing limbs.

"Poor fellows, we have no idea what horrors they've been through, almost being burned alive as their planes were shot down or having been the main target of a bomb," said Smitty.

"Our petty concerns pale in comparison to theirs. We will be forever in debt to those guys, and the ones who've sacrificed their lives," Harry added.

"I don't think they're going to care whether we have our sheet music or not," Bill remarked. "Shh—the speeches are starting."

After Air Marshal Johnson officially opened the new wing, they filed in for supper, and the dance afterward. They were told not to react in any way to the patients' severe injuries or facial disfigurement.

Bournemouth, Sept. 7, 1945 [excerpt]

Dearest Helen,

On Wednesday we went out to East Grimstead on that hospital job I told you about. We marched from the town to the hospital and back about three miles. The hospital is for fellows with severe burns and needing plastic surgery. I've never seen more horrible cases than were at that dance. One fellow had both ears burned off also his nose and his whole face was a mass of scars. I don't know how some of them lived through it. I woke up in a sweat the next morning thinking about them. The townspeople are warned not to stare at them as they [the patients] *are encouraged to walk around the streets as though there was nothing the matter with them. We got back to London at 4 a.m. on the back of a truck after a gruelling ride.*

We went up to London on Tuesday and I went to the Beaver Club and bought you a coin bracelet made out of threepenny bits. I hope you like it.

Take care of yourself darling.

All my love honey.

x x x x x x Harry

21
When Will He Return?

An hour never passes but I think of you
An hour never passes but I miss you too
Every day from dawning till the moon rides low
You're beside me, darling, everywhere I go

"An Hour Never Passes," by Jimmy Kennedy

The war in Europe had been over for three months and Helen was becoming anxious to know when Harry would return. In his letter of July 29, 1945, he said that he thought he would be home by Christmas, but that it all depended on the number of troops coming back, the spaces available on the ships, and the point system, where each person was given a priority ranking—those with the most points would come home sooner. Harry was subject to the decisions of the officers in charge and did not really know for sure.

Helen was having difficulty keeping her spirits up.

Toronto, Aug. 4, 7, 1945[excerpts]

My Own Darling Harry,

I was so happy to receive your letter today.. I just had to answer it tonight, but I haven't very much to tell you. Gee! It sounds more definite now as to when you're coming. It's so nice to think about it; I've always been afraid to. If it's just four more months, that isn't so long. Yes, it will be two years Monday since I've seen you; and I can still feel you when I pretend! There's something to it, I know that, darling, and I know what you mean when you explain it.

Well, honey, I hope you haven't heard anything to contradict that last report. If it's true, we're only about four months apart, so don't uncross those fingers. The Army Personnel from the Ile de France arrived today and the R.C.A.F. tomorrow.[1] Our Department [at the TTC] *chartered twelve buses to Hamilton and outside points* [i.e. where the ship was docking]. *They say Mayor Saunders* [mayor of Toronto] *has been down to meet every train so far to welcome the boys. At first he had a long speech, but he's gradually shortening it. I haven't been down to the Coliseum* [where the troop trains are coming in] *yet.*

Love Helen

The annual Canadian National Exhibition in Toronto was suspended from 1942 to 1946, as the Department of National Defence used the buildings for troop training and demobilization.

Veterans had been gathering at the Coliseum starting in May 1945, when the first boats began to arrive from England. The

---

1   Built after the First World War, the SS *Île de France* was a French ocean liner that was used as a troop ship during the Second World War, then, once the war ended, transported the soldiers back home.

returning soldiers expected on August 8, 1945, had come back on the *Queen Elizabeth* ocean liner to New York City, then had taken the train from there to Toronto.

The noise was deafening in the Coliseum as thousands of people filled the seats, anxiously awaiting the arrival of their loved ones. Others, such as Helen and her cousin Georgie, were there as supporters to welcome the battalions home.

Now that she was actually there, Helen wasn't sure it had been such a good idea to come. All she could think about was when Harry would return. However, she tried to put on a happy face and take part in the good cheer surrounding her.

Relatives were holding up "Welcome Home" signs, and the band struck up with "Hail, Hail, the Gang's All Here." A roar erupted when the soldiers marched into the huge arena.

Toronto, Aug. 9, 16, 1945[excerpts]

Darling Harry,

They finally persuaded me to go down to the Coliseum last night honey, and what excitement there was! An Air Force Band played when the 800 airmen marched in. They dropped their bags, looked around for their section, and lost no time in finding their relatives. You see the seats are divided with letters of the alphabet and the people seat themselves accordingly. It was a grand sight, but I knew I'd feel funny – you know exactly how I stood there spellbound. Our turn must come – it must. I see where they expect a slow-up again in repatriation, but they should crowd you in somewhere. Imagine some of them spending their seventh Christmas there – they shouldn't be asked to bear that.

Lynn [Helen's friend] *said she heard today they were transferring two big boats to the European run – that may speed things up a little. It takes time for all these changes though.*

All my love, Helen

* * *

It had been two years since Helen had seen her parents and younger siblings. So in September 1945, when it looked like Harry wouldn't be coming back for a while, she took the train to Saskatchewan to spend three weeks with them.

Not wanting to miss any of Harry's letters while she was away, Helen asked him to address his letters to Melfort, where her parents now lived. After two years of sending mail across the ocean, she could predict how long his letters might take to arrive.

When she arrived at the farm, Helen noticed that her father looked thinner and that her mother's hair was greyer. Her three younger sisters, Jean, Velma, and Vivie, were so happy to have her back that they stayed home from school for two days to be with her. Helen helped them with their homework and they told her all about their "big problems." She was settling back into family life on the farm.

"How do you like Toronto now, Helen?" her mother asked, looking up from sewing a patch on Jack's pants.

"Well, it's quite different from here, that's for sure. There's lots to do —going to the movies, going shopping, seeing my cousins. Never a dull moment," Helen said. She was embroidering a table set for her hope chest.

"You're quite the city girl now."

"Oh, Mother, in spite of all that, I do miss everyone here, especially you and the girls," she sobbed, putting down her handiwork and giving her mother a hug.

Just then, her father came in from town, after stopping at the co-op and the post office.

Tearing herself from her mother's arms, Helen asked him, "Is there a letter for me?"

"I think I did see a blue airmail letter. . . . Now where did I put it?" He smiled, checking his pockets. "Oh, here it is."

Snatching it from his hands, Helen ran upstairs and closed the door.

Her parents looked at each other.

"I guess there's no use wasting our breath trying to persuade her to come back home," her mother sighed, picking up her sewing.

Louisa and daughter Helen Reeder in Saskatchewan

Melfort, Sask. Sept. 14 - 21, 1945 [excerpts]

My Sweetheart Harry,

My Dad gave me your letter of 10th at noon. He had it in his pocket and it was a bit crumpled [it's torn and wrinkled]. *He pretended he lost it for a few minutes, just to see the expression on my face. Maybe he doesn't quite know how precious they are to me.*

I wasn't expecting one so soon, hope you are getting mine now honey. It would be terrible to go without a <u>wee</u> bit of sunshine. I'm so glad they [her letters] *cheer you up a little. If I could only give more of myself!*

Yes, darling, I'm enjoying my holidays but don't ask me what I'm doing besides eating and sleeping. Well, last night Ray [Helen's brother who was in the RCAF] *and I were out for supper to one of my girl friends. She was just married last November and seems very happy. They are building their own home this fall. Ray went overseas with her brother-in-law, so we all had lots to talk about. I didn't intend to do anything exciting when I came and anyway, how could I sweetheart without you? I mean that sweet. Eleanor has been home for a couple of months, and is going back to Vancouver soon, so I'll have to see her too.*

My sisters didn't go to school for two days because they wanted to stay home and talk to me. They had me helping them with Art and Arithmetic last night. Art was always my weak subject.

They've all decided what they want to study for already. [Jean became a nurse, Velma became a teacher and Vivie went into accounting.]

Jim [Helen's brother who was in the Navy] *has his discharge now and enrolled for an eight months' course in the University. He leaves on Oct. 1st.*

It's quite a change for me when I don't have to go to work and I'll try to get a good rest as you told me.

I just heard at noon that another 4,000 had landed at Quebec. One of these days. .

Mother and I just had a long talk, mostly about us. They like to know what we are planning, they don't understand that it's hard to plan through letters. Parents are always thinking of your welfare whether at home or away it seems. Yours do too, I know that. I bet your Mother is expecting you any day now. I'll probably get her answer to my letter the beginning of next week.

I worked some this morning, cleaned upstairs and dusted. When my sisters are here they won't let me do anything.

They lunch between meals here, but I won't eat. My brothers think they know why and they're always kidding me. Well, so what, I can't gain weight.

I'm embroidering a table set now; four place mats and a centre-piece. It's a good pastime, and I keep everything.

I've been sitting here long enough I guess, so will close. I'm saving all my kisses for you. Goodbye darling. My best love,

Helen xxxx

22
Those Bits of Paper

Night and day, you are the one
Only you 'neath the moon or under the sun
Whether near to me or far
It's no matter, darling, where you are
I think of you day and night

"Night and Day," by Cole Porter

Over the previous two years Harry and Helen had kept their love alive through their letters to each other, with Helen writing about four or five times a week and Harry averaging about twice a week.

The Base Post Office of the Canadian Postal Corps in Ottawa handled, sorted, and sent letters and parcels overseas. In the early years of the war, the mail was transported by ship several times a week. In 1943, RCAF cargo planes were commissioned to transport the mail in an effort to speed up delivery. Some letters were sent as "airgraphs," photos of one-page letters that were reduced in size and developed on microfilm, which weighed less to send.[1] At the other end, they were printed onto paper and delivered. Among the approximately 600 blue airmail letters that Helen and Harry wrote to each other, about twenty were airgraphs.

The couple had been having a hard time keeping their morale up during the last few months and encouraged each other to keep writing.

Helen Reeder mailing a letter to Harry Culley

Toronto, Oct.18, 1945 [excerpt]

Darling Harry,

I just took a few of your letters out of my billfold, you should see my file, honey. I shall have to get a bigger holder for them or something and they should be filed according to date, but oh! that would take me so long. I'll count them though one

---

1   "The Morale Department," by D'Arcy Jenish, *Legion Magazine*

of these days, just for fun. I hope you'll be able to find room for all of mine when you pack up.

I just stopped to count them – 205 to be exact. That's about two a week, so you have kept up a good record I must say, considering the fact that you dislike writing letters in the first place. But you did it for me and that's wonderful. . . .

All my love dearest, Helen

Bournemouth, Oct. 25, 1945 [excerpt]

My Darling Sweetheart Helen,

Received your letters of 16th & 18th this morning and I must say I was looking forward to them during our stay in London. I have to laugh at you counting my letters darling. I think it would take me hours to count yours, but I have every one of them. Smitty says I'm silly to keep them because I never seem to have time to read them over again but all our love has been built up around those bits of paper and I couldn't bear to tear them up. I think I've done pretty well in writing two a week considering the hectic life we lead over here . . .

Love, Harry

Toronto, Nov. 9, 1945 [excerpt]

My Darling Harry,

I had a funny dream about you last night, honey, and I'm wondering how you are. Silly of me – I guess. There's a slight delay in the mail again, it must be that post office over there. Sometimes they are post-marked four days after you mail them. There shouldn't be much reason for that now, should there?

Letters are just as important now as they ever were. That was sweet what you said about our letters. We'll bind them up, and read them over about twenty years from now – or would we enjoy doing that then? Anyway, it's a nice thought. . . So long again, sweet, your love is always with me.

Yours forever, Helen xxxxx

Harry Culley writing to Helen Reeder

23
The Waiting Game

You must remember this
A kiss is just a kiss, a sigh is just a sigh
The fundamental things apply
As time goes by

"As Time Goes By," by Herman Hupfeld

The RCAF No. 3 Personnel Reception Centre Band had been putting in the time in Bournemouth until it was to return to Canada by playing in the bandstand in the lower gardens near the Pavilion, playing at the Westover (formerly a skating rink), playing dances for the American GIs, marching in parades, performing in lunchtime concerts at the sergeants' mess and in tea dances at the Red Cross Club, and travelling to London for official ceremonies, where band members no longer had to worry about dropping bombs.

At first Martin Boundy (the head music director for the RCAF) said they would be going home in April 1946. Then that date was changed to January or February 1946. Harry was reluctant to tell Helen, for fear of the date being changed again, but decided to anyway.

Bournemouth, Oct. 12, 13, 1945 [excerpts]

My Darling Helen,

I wrote you yesterday that they promised we'd be home by April, but last night at the Westover, Boundy's right hand man was talking to us and he felt sure we'd be going home in Jan. or Feb. – so that's a little better isn't it sweetheart?

Hunt's band and what's left of the #1 band came down here yesterday and we have to practise marching for a W.D. inspection by the Queen in Buckingham Palace next weekend I think it is. The combined bands will make a band of 54 pieces and I was hoping to evade it as there are always too many clarinets, but I didn't succeed. Most of us are pretty sloppy on parade so we'll have to do a lot of fast slogging around the streets of B'mouth. I might even get a new uniform out of it as they want us all to look smart! We even have to rehearse Sun. afternoon!!

Well darling, I'm in the middle of six nights of dances in a row, even Sunday night, so I haven't much free time. The 1ˢᵗ alto man decided he'd like to try tenor again so I'll be playing alto for awhile. I'll be glad of the change.

I should be able to save another $1,000 between now and then if I keep working four nights a week, if that's any consolation. We'll have a bit of cash to start with when we do finally settle down. Oh happy day! Mother expects me home on every boat and it's so hard to explain to her as she doesn't realize the situation and I'm probably to blame too. Well, I can't worry about her too. You take up all my thoughts darling and it almost breaks my *heart to tell you when I realize how long you've been waiting now. If we can get a fresh grip on ourselves it shouldn't seem too long – or should it? I can just hear you say it's been too long now, and I agree with you.*

The boys who were on the Continent have some terrific stories to tell about the black market dealing in France and Belgium. They got a shilling apiece for cigarettes over there! One fellow bought a new French clarinet for 2000 cigarettes which would cost him about $7, the clarinet would cost at least $200 at home. One guy bought a fur coat for his wife. They nearly ate themselves to death in Denmark (Copenhagen), they had all the eggs and beef steak they could eat in restaurants. They travelled all over in open trucks but that was the worst part of it. If we had any idea that we were going over for Christmas I'd start buying up coffee beans over here by the bushel and do business in a big way, but nothing has been said about it. They saw the ruins of Kiel (a naval base in Germany) and Hamburg, but Paris is the city that knocked them out the most. I sure would like to see it.

Well darling, I'll have to close now, but I thought I'd let you know I should be home in Jan. or Feb. at the latest. I see the Queen Elizabeth [ocean liner] *is going to carry Canadians for a couple of months. That might make a difference to us I hope!*

Good bye for now dearest. All my love & kisses forever angel.

Harry xxxxx

Love in the Air

Toronto, Oct. 23, 1945

My Own Darling Harry,

I have been getting two letters together lately, honey – not that I mind. They were dated 12th and 13th. I can't say I felt elated after reading the latest, but still we might have known you'd be about the last to come. No, I'm not sorry you're in the Band, because there are many advantages to it. If you had to stay there five or six months and just put in time then it would be just too, too bad. This is the only way to look at it I say to myself, and it is a consolation to know we'll have savings through your efforts. You can say that again; we'll be a happy pair. It has been a long wait, and it would have been hard to wait if we had been together. In that case, would we?? [i.e. have married]

Another thing I have to ask you tonight, and don't forget to answer right back. We're thinking of getting you a signet ring for your birthday – sorry we have to tell you but we want your size. So your Mother would like you to go into a jeweller and get the size of the finger on which you want to wear it, and also, how would you like the initials, raised, printed or otherwise? please designate. We want to send it, so don't tell us not to bother honey.

Well, I guess all that parading and rehearsing will be over. How long were you in London? Was this after our Prime Minister lunched with the King? I hope you were close enough to catch a good glimpse of the Queen. I'm sure you'll remember those important moments, even though you are included against your will. Did you get a new uniform?

I was downtown yesterday on my off day, and let's see – what did I buy? a black hat with sequins in front to wear over my forehead or back. By the way, my coat was delivered today and I tried them both on together and they look smart. I'm wearing my other coat to work and will keep this one nice. Then I got a plain green wool dress for work too, but no blouse yet. That wasn't bad for an afternoon, was it? Considering the way I walked through the crowds as usual.

I was interrupted, Georgie just phoned. She asked about you and I had to go into detail – you know how it is.

I'll have a few more dateless nights. I'll feel like a different person when I go out and forget all but our little world and the two of us, oh darling. Now it's goodnight.

All my love, Helen xxxxx

P.S. I just heard about your parade on the news and your Band was mentioned.

* * *

During the war many British women contributed as part of the armed forces. They joined the Women's Auxiliary Air Force, for instance, or if they were from the upper classes, they volunteered their time doing charitable and humanitarian work. Lady Frances Ryder helped to organize a hospitality service whereby RCAF personnel could enjoy their leaves by staying in private homes in Britain. Between 1943 and July 1945, approximately 35,000 members of the RCAF took part in this program.

To acknowledge the work that Lady Ryder did for the Canadian soldiers stationed in England, the RCAF held a special air force tea dance in her honour at the Royal Bath Hotel in Bournemouth.

As the band members were unpacking their instruments, Ken came over to talk to Harry.

"Are you feeling blue?" he asked.

"Yes, why?"

"Here, this should make you feel better," he said, handing Harry three letters.

"Wow! Quite a bonanza—from my father, mother, and Helen. How did you get them?"

"On the way in, Ossie told me to give them to you."

Harry quickly scanned the letter from Helen, then tuned up. As they started to play, Harry found himself making a lot of mistakes.

"What's up?" Ossie asked him between numbers.

"I can't help thinking about Helen and how swell she is. I guess I shouldn't have read that letter right before the dance."

Ossie smiled. "Better keep your mind on the music, or Lady Ryder will be upset."

"You're right; she deserves to be honoured. Smitty and I stayed at homes in Oxford arranged through her."

When the dance was over, Steve announced to them in a low voice that they needed to report back at 10 a.m. the next morning for an important announcement.

"Great, maybe finally we'll get some news about when we can go home," said Smitty. "I'm beginning to think they want to keep us here indefinitely to provide free entertainment for all of their official ceremonies."

"I know, we're almost busier now than when the war was on—I've played sixteen jobs out of eighteen days already this month," Harry replied.

They all went home wondering what the news would be.

Bournemouth, Dec. 8, 1945

Joanne Culley

My Darling Helen,

The axe fell yesterday and with it went my head! I'm being posted to Torquay [a town 120 km west of Bournemouth] *on Monday with 9 other boys from our band, eleven men are going home in the very near future and 8 are staying here to play at the Westover. Bill and Smitty will be staying, naturally I expected to be staying with them but, oh no. There's just as much dance work down there and they get paid for them but I don't think they get a living out allowance.*

Anyway, darling I have some good news for you – it's only for six weeks and then I'll be going home – isn't that wonderful? Now you can start counting the weeks instead of the months! It's all over on Feb. 1st according to Boundy. I sent the address to Mother to-day by wire. It's "R" depot RCAF Torquay Band, England. Gosh I hate leaving here especially when I think of all the junk we have to take – we have to make a couple of changes to get to Torquay and it's an 8 hour trip from here so it will be a tiresome day. Just one more unnecessary trip! Oh well, just six more weeks of it and Steve seemed pretty definite about it. He and the bunch should get home around Christmas or shortly after.

This is the coldest day we've had yet and it started to snow a bit this morning but it didn't amount to anything; the channel looks pretty rough too. I wonder how it will be in February!! Well sweet, the way they've got those ships running I can't see how it could be any longer than six weeks. There are fewer than 10,000 airmen over here now and they're rushing them through here to get them home for Christmas.

So that's the bombshell that dropped yesterday darling. The ones under 80 [points] *had almost given up hope of any action being taken until after Christmas but they are happy about it now. We're all getting together Sunday night for a final drinking party so I guess there'll be a few of them staggering around. There's only two of us that drink going to Torquay but I don't expect to have any time free when I get there for that especially with Christmas dances coming up.*

*Well, sweetheart, you've waited a long time to hear something definite and according to this news I should be home a few weeks sooner than I expected and I sure hope they go plenty fast until Feb. 1*st*.*

I'll close for now darling and write when I get to Torquay. I'll be seeing you soon, sweetheart.

All my love, Harry xxxxxxxx

RCAF dance band, Al Smith on piano on right, Harry
Culley second from right on saxophones

Harry was upset to be uprooted from Bournemouth, where they had been stationed for the past two years, and posted to Torquay. He and nine others from the Bournemouth band had been victims of the military bureaucratic decision-making process. Harry's good friends Smitty and Bill were not among those transferred.

To top off Harry's dissatisfaction, once they got there, it seemed that the bandmaster at Torquay, didn't need them, leaving Harry and the others confused as to the reason they were moved.

"Why on earth Steve sent us down here, I'll never know," Harry grumbled as they waited in line at the Labour Exchange.

"I don't think Leroy even knew we were coming—he certainly doesn't have any work for us," said Frank, the trombone player.

"I don't know about you, but I can't live on three shillings a day," said Harry.

"Hopefully, we can get some other work here. The guy I was talking to at the canteen said there are lots of jobs around now."

"Not at the post office, though; I tried there yesterday and the local kids have that place all sewn up," said Harry.

"Next!" boomed the official behind the counter.

"We've been sent down from Bournemouth and need some temporary work, if you have it," offered Frank.

The fellow looked them up and down. "RCAF? I'm afraid it isn't legal for Canadians to work in England."

"I see," said Frank.

"However," continued the official, as he leaned over the counter whispering, "I heard that the Twillings and Cranfields construction companies need help—you could try there. Here are their addresses. If you have any trouble, come back here."

The two headed off eagerly and were hired on at the first place, at about 1.8 halfpennies, or thirty-five cents, an hour.

"Well, that's good," said Harry. "We start tomorrow; that's better than doing nothing, and will harden up our muscles."

"How about we take the rest of the day off and walk over to Paignton, to see the Singer Sewing Machine Estate?"[1] Frank suggested.

"Sounds great."

Torquay, England, Dec. 13, 15, 1945 [excerpts]

Dearest Helen,

I'm almost too tired to write you to-night, darling, but I'm making a supreme effort. As you know 4 of us are helping Britain build houses for a week and we're doing all the heavy labour. Two of us were mixing cement all day yesterday by hand and wheeling it up an incline on planks. Boy, is that ever tough on the arms & shoulders! I'm glad we only had a half day to-day. I wouldn't

---

1   The Oldway Mansion at Paignton was purchased by Isaac Merritt Singer, who founded the Singer Sewing Machine Company, around 1871. His son, Paris Singer, remodelled the mansion in the early 1900s in the style of the Palace of Versailles

have been much use this afternoon. I'm hoping the stiffness leaves my arms by Monday. It won't do me any harm anyway and I'm really ready for bed by 9:30 because we have to get up by 6:30 a.m. Anything for a laugh eh? I never thought I'd use my rubber boots but ploughing around in Devonshire red clay makes them indispensable. It's still very mild so a sweater coat and sweater is enough to keep me warm.

Well sweetheart, it's been a full week since I heard from you last and I wonder when my mail is going to locate me? You'd think a week would be sufficient wouldn't you? I'm sure you're keeping well darling. It's awfully hard for me to realize it's only ten days to Christmas but I guess you and the family are in the thick of it right now. Little kids go around the hotels here singing Christmas carols for pennies but it's hard to get the Christmas spirit in drizzly weather and away from the people you love.

Yesterday we walked to Paignton – a suburb of Torquay – to the Singer Sewing Machine Estate. It's taken over by the Knights of Columbus and is really terrific. The home itself looks like a palace and there is a golf course, bowling green and tennis courts on the estate. There's a good service club not far from where we're billeted and we get all the chocolate bars we need.

Well, sweetheart, I suppose I'll be even lonelier this Christmas being away from the boys – and you of course! . . . Leroy is really pulling to get the ones he doesn't need home as soon as possible in January and then there will just be the dance men left.

They're getting ready to show a film here so I'll probably stick around and see it, they show one every night here. I haven't any one to have a beer with me any more, so I guess this will be a dry birthday this time.

Well, sweetheart, I must close now as I'm getting a bit sleepy. I hope you have a nice Christmas, darling. I might go down to B'mouth for Christmas if I get a chance and see Smitty and Bill. Be seeing you soon, sweet.

All my love, xxxxxx Harry

Toronto, Dec. 20, 1945

My Darling Harry,

The postman was about two hours late this morning, but he brought me your two letters of 11th and 13th so it was all right.

I was glad to have your recent report confirmed [i.e. about when he is coming home.] *I was afraid you may have been misinformed as you had been a few times before. But it actually sounds good, sweet.*

I can imagine how you feel being set down there [i.e. at Torquay], *practically by yourself after having all the other boys around, but it isn't a permanent move, so just take it in your stride honey. I doubt if Steve could give a logical reason for singling you out. It's one big shuffle this time.*

I hope they get those under 80's off [i.e. those who have under 80 points, who have priority on the boats returning home], *then it will be your turn.*

Just because some of them aren't doing anything, that shouldn't be a reason for sending them first. They can get busy and <u>exercise</u> their muscles like you are. By the way, how was it? You wouldn't recommend it for an everyday job, would you? I bet you ate two meals in one after the first day.

Love, Helen

24
Christmas 1945

I'm in the mood for love
Simply because you're near me
Funny, but when you're near me
I'm in the mood for love

"I'm in the Mood for Love," lyrics by Dorothy
Fields, music by Jimmy McHugh

Being employed at the Toronto Transportation Commission,
Helen had to work day, night, weekend, and holiday shifts,
as the buses and streetcars ran into the early hours of the
morning. But she didn't mind working odd hours, as it filled in
the time until Harry's return.

On Christmas Day 1945, Helen worked the day shift and
went over to Harry's parents' apartment for supper, arriving at
about 6:30 p.m.

"I'm sorry to be so late; I had to wait a long time for the
Bloor streetcar—they're on a reduced schedule because of
Christmas," she explained, taking off her coat.

"Not to worry, we've been snacking on peanuts and pretzels,
and playing with David," said Harry Sr.

Helen rushed over to the baby, who was sitting on a blanket near the tree. He gave a little squeal when he saw her.

"Merry Christmas, my little man, and what did Santa bring you?" Helen cooed, giving him a kiss.

"He did quite well, didn't you, love?" said his mother Elaine. "A little toy elephant on wheels that he can pull when he starts to walk, some blocks, and a jack-in-the-box—but he puts everything in his mouth! He must be getting a new tooth. We've been trying to distract him from the little Santas on the tree."

Helen looked up at the felt-and-wire Santas perched jauntily on the branches of the most beautifully decorated tree she had ever seen. Large, colourful lights were set amidst star tin reflectors. Atop them sat fan decorations with blades that spun around from the heat of the lights. Finally, she felt that she was into the Christmas spirit.

"You just missed Ross—he ate early and went off to play with Bert Niosi at the Royal York," said Ida, bustling in from the kitchen. "Dinner's ready now, so let's all eat."

After the sumptuous feast, Ida sat down to play some Christmas carols on the piano while the others gathered around. As she sang the old familiar words, Helen's mind wandered across the ocean, wondering if Harry was doing the same thing.

It was quite late when she got up to go home. But when Ida insisted she stay overnight, she found herself sleeping in Harry's old room.

Toronto, Dec. 26, 1945 [excerpts]

My Sweetheart Harry,

Well, It's all over honey, and I haven't gone home yet, isn't that terrible? You see, I worked yesterday, and I came here for dinner. When I talked of going home about eleven your Mother started coaxing me to stay for the night. I wasn't going to and she started asking me for reasons why I wanted to go home and said this was my last chance, etc. etc. so I finally gave in. I tried out your bed, it's pretty soft. All your suits are hanging up waiting for you. Gee! honey, it was a nice feeling to sleep where you'll be sleeping.

Did you enjoy yourself fairly well, sweet? I hope you went to Bournemouth with the boys. We were thinking about you. I wish you could have seen the table when we sat down and had your share of the goodies. The turkey was very tasty. Did you have some?

Your letter of 15th came Monday, I wanted one before Christmas. I bet you didn't feel much like writing with your sore muscles. I do appreciate your effort. It's no fun getting up at 6:30 is it? It shouldn't take much longer than a week for the mail to get to you. You should be getting it all right now.

I did well for presents – a scarf from you, a nightgown from your Mother and Dad, white slippers from Elaine and Ross and a box of powder from Santa. Mother made me a nice coloured bag with wooden handles, also had a bridge table set, hankies, stationery and candy, so I did pretty well didn't I?

We had drizzly rain, just like you've been having, and two days before it was five below. Changes fast, doesn't it?

Those little kids sound cute singing carols. They have quite a nice choir at Wychwood [Presbyterian Church], *and I enjoyed listening to the carols Sunday night.*

I go in at 4:30 so that's how I happen to have the time off now. Oh yes, darling, your cable came on the 20th [the cable sending her Christmas wishes] *and it was dated 18th – quick service, wasn't it? Thanks for your loving wishes. I can do with all of them from you.*

Well, so long my sweetheart, wouldn't it be super if I could see you the first month of this year?

I love you and I'm yours. Helen

* * *

At Christmastime Harry decided to go back to Bournemouth to see his bandmates along with three others who had been sent to Torquay. As soon as the bus got in, they headed down to the Beach Café, where their former dance band was playing.

During the break, Ken looked up to see Harry in the audience and went down to greet him.

"Good to see you, Harry. How are things over at Torquay?"

"Not bad if you like construction work; that's all there is to do over there."

"Well, the band hasn't been the same without you. Listen, can you sit in with us? We have to play at the bowling green and those songs don't seem any good without you, especially 'I'm in the Mood for Love.'"

"Sure, I'd love to. I hope I'm not too out of practice."

"Good to see you, Harry!" Smitty beamed as he came over to shake his good friend's hand.

"Smitty's been in the sauce a bit too much lately—I think he misses his best buddy," commented Ken.

Harry gave Smitty a warm slap on the back. "Well, I don't have anyone to drink with over in Torquay either, so let's make up for lost time."

"R"Depot R.C.A.F. Band, Overseas, Dec. 25, 1945

My Dearest Helen,

Needless to say, I've been thinking about you more than ever to-day darling, and the more I think about you the more lonesome I get. I've been putting the clock back five hours all day and have been trying to imagine what you would be doing. This has been the quietest Christmas I've spent over here as I had practically nothing to drink outside of a couple of mugs of beer at noon with my turkey. I scrounged two meals out of the Bowling Green at noon to-day and they were both wonderful. I never saw a menu like it, there was literally everything on it from soup to nuts and of course I made a pig of myself, but I was so hungry. I went over to the Westover to-night intending to have a dance but didn't. I just sat around for a couple of hours and listened to the Streamliners – it's a nice band. The weather was perfect this afternoon and I could hardly realize it was Christmas. I still can't imagine Christmas without snow.

I think I'll stay in B'mouth until the 3rd of Jan. unless they wire me to come back before that. I have three jobs this week which will pay my expenses for the week, so that's not bad.

I wish I could give you some more news on when I expect to get back darling but I haven't heard a thing. They're closing all these stations up pretty soon now so until then I guess we're frozen. Everybody will be glad to see Boundy gone this week, but I don't know whether he's to blame for the hold-up or not. The other fellows expect to leave next month some time. I'm afraid I'll faint when they tell me I'm going home at last, I hope you don't when you get the telegram sweetheart.

Well, angel, I'm very tired to-night (maybe because I ate so much) so will close for now with all my love and kisses forever,

Yours Harry xxxxx

25
Last Letters and the Long Trip Home

Long ago and far away, I dreamed a dream one day
And now that dream is here beside me
Long the skies were overcast, but now the clouds have
passed
You're here at last

"Long Ago and Far Away," lyrics by Ira
Gershwin, music by Jerome Kern

After enjoying the Christmas break in Bournemouth with all
of their old friends, Harry and the others were ordered back
to Torquay, where they worked at labouring jobs, attended
concerts, went sightseeing along the coast, and generally put
in the time.

On January 19, 1946, they played their bandmaster Steve
and others onto the train at the Torquay railway station. Harry
was becoming despondent, seeing so many of his comrades
going home.

On January 21, Harry decided to take matters into his own
hands. He arranged to have his leave in London so that he could

go right to the top, to nail down when his turn would come. Four days later, at a meeting with Sergeant Worthylake, Harry learned he was a "cinch to go home." Upon hearing the news, he rushed down to the Rainbow Corner, the American Red Cross Club at 23 Shaftesbury Avenue near Piccadilly Circus, and booked a call to Helen.

"Is there a Harry Culley here?" the sergeant's voice boomed through the room.

"Yes, that's me," Harry said excitedly.

"Your call is connected—you can take it in my office."

Harry rushed over to the desk and lifted up the phone. The line crackled with static.

"Hello?"

"Is that you, Harry?"

Her voice sounded as far away as she actually was, but he knew it was Helen.

"Yes, it's me—how are you, darling?"

"Fine, but what about you—do you have any news?"

"Yes, I've just been approved to go home on February 15!"

"Oh, that's wonderful! I can't believe it!"

"Well, it's true. Finally, after all these long months. How is the weather there now?"

"It's quite cold here—below zero, in fact. Winter has set in."

"Well, I don't care how cold it is, you'll keep me warm, darling. I can't wait to hold you in my arms again."

"Me too. I hope it's not too stormy on the North Atlantic; the ships have been taking about six days or so."

"Yes, that sounds right. I can hardly hear you."

"I can't hear you very well either, but I love you and I can hardly wait to see you again."

"I love you too, dear. Bye for now."

"R" Depot Band RCAF Overseas, Jan. 27, 1946

My Darling Helen,

Well, it was a short three minutes wasn't it sweetheart? They can communicate with the moon faster than it took them to get through to you but it was worth waiting six hours and £3 to hear your voice again. It was very clear but kept fading away and I couldn't tell when you were finished speaking. I could tell you were very excited at the beginning darling. I put the original call in at 1 p.m. your time at your home but the lines weren't operating; when New York accepted the call through there I gave them your business number. About 11:30 p.m. here I told the fellow I'd take the call from the Club and it wasn't 10 minutes after I got here that they got through to you. After that I went straight up to bed with nothing but you on my mind darling. I dreamed everybody came over here to see me—that is everybody but you—how about that!

Yes, when Worthylake told me I'd be leaving next month I rushed down to Shaftsbury Ave. to reserve a wire to you sweet. The operator said I could phone right away to New York but the Canadian wires were never dependable as I soon discovered.

I'm leaving on the 9:30 to-morrow for Lincoln and I should be back the same night. I sure hope those books [the volumes of Household Words by Charles Dickens that he saw in a used bookstore there] *are up there yet, but maybe I'm expecting too much. It's much milder now so it won't be any hardship travelling. I shivered when you told me it was below zero darling. I went for a short stroll along the embankment before the concert to-day and it was very nice but awfully lonely darling. I had a glimpse of St. Paul's from Ludgate Circus and*

*went up Fleet St. to the Aldwich—but you don't
know one street from another do you darling. I do
so much wish you were here angel. I was opposite
St. Dunstan's Church on Fleet and there are two
iron figures in a tower who strike the hour and ½
hour on two bells and wiggle their heads. It was
so funny to watch.*

*Well sweet I must close this before my eyes close
before I finish. I heard you say you love me angel
and I'll never forget it as long as I live.*

My love is yours. Harry xxxxxx

This was Harry's last letter from England.

* * *

On January 31, Harry and the others returned to Torquay,
where few military personnel remained. Corporal Hart had
all their clearances signed and they were told to leave for the
RCAF airbase at Topcliffe in North Yorkshire the next day. "Oh
Joy!" Harry wrote in his diary.

They loaded their kit bags, then left again on the midnight
train back to London. They reached Paddington Station at 5:30
a.m., spent four hours in the city, and then departed from Kings
Cross Station at 9:30 a.m. They arrived in Topcliffe at 4 p.m. to
go through the official decommissioning process.

In his diary, Harry wrote, "We drew blankets and walked 1
mile to AMQ 7. The longest mile I ever walked, ready for bed
at 6 p.m." (They wouldn't have slept at all the previous night,
except for a bit on the train.)

On February 3, Harry wrote, "Parade at 9:30 a.m. and 1:30
p.m. Kit inspected."

* * *

Toronto, Feb. 5, 1945[excerpts]

My Darling Harry,

I was happy all over again last night when I received yours of 27th, to know that you heard everything I said – I was so afraid you wouldn't. I didn't hear you say good bye darling. You never did like saying that, did you?

I hope you get this in ten days, and also all the others before you leave. I don't know just when to stop, because I haven't heard it confirmed about 17th. It wouldn't be any fun getting them [her letters] *after you got back here, but I wouldn't care about a trifling thing like that I guess. The last week I'll be lost* [i.e. the week he is on the ship and she cannot write to him] *and going around in a daze. Well, I'm praying that you'll get here safely, and that all will be well with us.*

They are planning to have "twice a day" mail delivery next month, so they'll have all the ex-postmen back, not that it will do us any good at this late date. I could have had lots of your letters a day sooner if that had been in effect.

If you're still going to leave on the date mentioned, I shouldn't write after next Sunday, [Feb. 10], *should I? After that, I'll begin to realize that you're really coming. It's a week already since you phoned me; I was thinking of it last night.*

I've cleaned my room as best I could. It needs redecorating, that's why it's hard to see much improvement. I washed the curtains, waxed the floors, etc. I hope you find it comfortable enough to relax in and enjoy yourself – with me here of course! It's a long walk, [i.e. from St. Clair Avenue] *and I expect to hear complaints about that* [from him].

I hope they see fit to send you on the next trip of the Queen Elizabeth. It would be nicer to dock at New York than Halifax anyway, wouldn't it? The Queen Mary is all set to bring British War Brides.

When you come in we'll be as close to the front in Section "C" as we can get so look for us there. And remember, get there the quickest way possible.

Yes, I guess I should have joined the W.D.'s and gone over there with you, honey, or maybe I could have stowed away. Anything to have shared some of the times you had, but I guess it just wasn't meant to be.

Do you have to reserve wires, sweet? Will you send me one when you're leaving? Just before you go aboard. I'll be waiting for it. I know I'll single you out of that crowd so quickly – be seeing you.

Best love, Helen xxxxx

This was Helen's last letter.

* * *

On February 14, the band members took the train from Thirsk, the nearest railway station, down to Southampton on the southern coast of England, where they boarded the *Queen Elizabeth* ocean liner.[1] On February 15, a tugboat pulled them out of the docks.

---

1   The *Queen Elizabeth* was a luxury ship that was used to transport troops during the Second World War. During that time, the ship carried 750,000 military personnel and sailed approximately 500,000 miles.

RCAF band members going home on the Queen Elizabeth

Six days later, on February 20, 1946, just as Helen had predicted, they arrived in the harbour at New York City, where a ferry took them to their trains. Harry's aunt Catherine and cousin Betty met him at the station, the first relatives to greet him in North America after his two and a half years away, and they had a visit prior to his boarding the train to Toronto.

Harry on left, Ossie in middle, aboard Queen Elizabeth

* * *

Helen could hardly contain her excitement when February 21 finally arrived, the day she had been awaiting for two and a half years. Arriving at the Coliseum on the grounds of the Canadian

National Exhibition, she saved two seats for Harry's parents in Section C, for Culley. Ida and Harry Sr. arrived shortly after.

When she saw the long line of servicemen entering the building, Helen frantically scanned each face until she alighted on Harry's. She started waving her arms frantically and calling out his name. At that moment, he spotted her and ran toward her, while she left her seat, pushing others aside as she moved quickly down the aisle. When they finally reached each other, they hugged so tightly they could hardly breathe. Helen started to cry, while all the time kissing him and saying his name. All those years of writing letters were finally over—he was really here in the flesh. Any doubts she had had about whether he still loved her vanished when she saw his face. Their love had indeed grown through the 609 letters they'd written to each other. Unlike their sad embrace at the train station before he left, this time there was joy at his safe return.

Ida patted Helen's shoulders gently and smiled, saying, "It's my turn."

Helen reluctantly tore herself away so that Harry could hug his parents.

"Welcome home, son, good job," said Harry Sr., embracing him.

"I can't believe I'm finally here—I've been dreaming of this moment ever since I left," marvelled Harry.

"Me too," replied Helen.

"Well, I've got some stew on the stove; let's go back to the apartment and hear all about your trip back," Ida remarked, wiping her eyes.

They all helped to carry his bags, and as they made their way slowly through the crowd toward the streetcars, Harry kept glancing sideways, smiling at Helen and thinking how beautiful she looked, amazed that she had waited for him all those years. Helen couldn't stop crying for joy, and apologized for making a fool of herself.

"No need to worry about that; I'm not going anywhere now," Harry said, squeezing her hand. He bent down and whispered in her ear, "I love you, honey."

"I love you too," she replied. Saying it out loud, instead of on paper, made it more real somehow. She didn't think there'd been a happier moment in all of her life. True love was like a rock, she thought, and she and Harry were granite.

* * *

Harry and Helen's wedding, June 5, 1946, Toronto

The happy couple spent the next few months making up for lost time. Somehow, even though they'd been apart for so long, Helen felt that she knew Harry better than when he'd left. Through the letters, she'd learned his innermost feelings, laughed at his antics, experienced the thrills of playing for the king and queen, and felt his anxiety about the future. They busied themselves with arranging their wedding, finding a place to live, and planning their lives together.

On June 5, 1946, with Harry's good friend Al Smith (Smitty) as best man and Helen's cousin Georgie Reeder as maid of honour, the couple married at Wychwood Presbyterian Church in Toronto. Friend Lynn Sprigg captured the wedding with her new 16-mm movie camera on colour Kodachrome (possibly one of the first wedding films). Telegrams arrived from relatives in the United States and Canada; everyone rejoiced at the happy ending to this long love story.

Helen continued working at the TTC until she got married, as the policy was that married women had to give up their jobs for the men returning from the war. However, she got a job as a secretary at Aerofilms, a new company that produced movies from the air, using technology developed during the war.

Upon his return, Harry played with several bands, including the Len Davis big band and the Norm Harris big band at the King Edward Hotel, where he played clarinet, as well as alto and tenor saxophone, and also learned to play the flute. The Harris band toured around southern Ontario, performing at dance pavilions and hotels.

As big band music faded in popularity during the 1950s and jobs in that field decreased, Harry went to work as an accountant at the Ontario Ministry of Community and Social Services. But as a member of the Toronto Musicians' Association, he continued to play music on weekends and on New Year's Eve for dances and concerts throughout his life. Upon retirement, he played in the Toronto Flute Choir and the New Horizons Band.

Together Harry and Helen raised two sons and a daughter. Helen worked part time while the children were growing up, then went back to work full time when the youngest entered high school, working as a secretary at the Ministry of Education, not having lost her typing skills.

Helen's cousin Georgie and bassist Bill didn't get together after all. Georgie married Al Johnson and they had two children. Harry's friend Al Smith became a teacher, first at high schools in Toronto, then as a professor of music at the University of Alberta in Edmonton. He received bachelor and master of music degrees from the University of Toronto and a doctorate in music from the University of Oregon. He married Elizabeth Hamill and had one daughter, Caroline. He died in 2012.

When Helen died in 1997, she and Harry had been married fifty-one years. Harry died in 2009.

Helen and Harry Culley (front), back (l to r) Harry Culley Sr., Georgie Reeder, Al Smith, Art Stagg

Bibliography

Canada's Weekly for the Forces. Ottawa:1939–1945.

Edgington, M. A. *Bournemouth and the Second World War, 1939–1945*. Bournemouth, England: Bournemouth Local Studies Publication, 1994.

Franklin, Stephen. *A Time of Heroes*. Toronto: Natural Science of Canada, 1977.

Hockey, Betty. *Command Performance*. England: P. M. Print Ltd., date unknown. (privately printed)

Hurst, Alan M. *The Canadian YMCA in World War II*. Toronto: National War Services Committee of the National Council of Young Men's Christian Associations of Canada, 1950.

Jenish, D'Arcy. "The Morale Department." *Legion Magazine*. Kanata, Ontario: Canvet Publications Ltd., July/August 2012.

Kennedy, John de Navarre. *History of the Department of Munitions and Supply: Canada in the Second World War*. Ottawa: E. Cloutier, King's Printer, 1950.

Kopstein, Jack and Ian Pearson. *The Heritage of Canadian Military Music*. St. Catharines, Ontario: Vanwell, 2002.

McFadden, Fred, Don Quinlan, and Rick Life. *Canada: The Twentieth Century.* Toronto: Fitzhenry & Whiteside, 1982.

McGrath, John. *The Other End of the Spear: The Tooth-to-Tail Ratio in Modern Military Operations.* Fort Leavenworth, Kansas: Combat Studies Institute Press, 2007.

Payne, Stephen R. *History of the Rockcliffe Airport Site: Home of the National Aviation Museum.* Ottawa: National Aviation Museum, 1999.

Websites

www.ddaymuseum.co.uk

www.members.shaw.ca/junobeach (Lane, D. W. "Juno Beach: The Canadians on D-Day")

www.canadianwarbrides.com

Acknowledgements

As is the case with many military personnel, my father did not speak much about his time overseas. I am grateful to Caroline Smith, whose father was Al Smith (Smitty), my father's good friend during the war. She confirmed our fathers' camaraderie, and shared with me some of his anecdotes, a few of which I have included in this book.

I would like to thank Les Allison, trumpet player in the RCAF No. 3 Personnel Reception Centre Band and Ken Smith and Judy Smith McLarty, daughter and son of George Smith, cornet player, for their help with names, photos and other details, and to Judy's husband for retouching the London parade photo which appears in Chapter 19. Les Smith, who served with the Royal Air Force in England and Italy throughout the war, along with his wife Edna, filled me in on events taking place during that time.

Many thanks to the Sevenish writers' group: Diana Mansell, Eileen Dunne, Dorothy Cox Rothwell, Rita Grimaldi, Linda Driscoll and Mary Gordon without whose encouragement and regular meetings this book would not have come to fruition. Thanks especially to Susan Stanton, Mary Gordon and to historian and author Alan Skeoch for their valuable suggestions on improving the manuscript. Thanks to Kath Lucas, who suggested the title and with whom I meet regularly for "writes." My book club members have been also been a continuing source of inspiration.

Thanks to my brothers, Brian and Norman Culley, and to my husband Michael McMurtry and sons Stephen and Peter for their support and encouragement. My aunts helped me with family history – Velma Hamm and Vivie Malcolm, as well as Beryl Reeder and Jean Goguillot, now deceased, and cousin Evelyn Stagg.

My visit to Bournemouth, England, was fruitful: Betty Hockey told me about the concert parties she helped to stage in the city during the war; historian Michael Phipp told me about events taking place there during the war; Hazel Randall at the City of Bournemouth informed me about the history of Canadian soldiers there and showed me the plaque dedicated to them at the Bournemouth Town Hall; the research staff at the Bournemouth Library, and journalist Jane Reader wrote an article about the my parents' letters for the *Bournemouth Daily Echo*.

Thanks to Dr. Stephen Harris, CD, Acting Director and Chief Historian at the Canadian Department of National Defence, Lara Andrews at the Canadian War Museum, and the helpful staff at the Library and Public Archives Canada, all of whom responded to my many queries thoroughly.

I would like to acknowledge the excellent instructors at the Trent University Creative Writing program: Mary Breen, Judy Fong Bates, and Jane Bow, as well as Diane Taylor, whose memoir-writing course helped me to get started.

Thanks to Dana Mills, Tim Plakolli, editor Smitha Srinivasa, designer Colin Parks, and the staff at FriesenPress for their attention to detail while shepherding the manuscript into book form.

An earlier version of this story, with photos, appears on the blog www.loveintheairww2letters.blogspot.ca.

A portion of the proceeds from this book will go to the Trent Valley Literacy Association and the Culley Scholarship Fund at the Royal Conservatory of Music in Toronto.

About the Author

Joanne Culley received her MA in English Literature from the University of Toronto. She is an award-winning writer and documentary producer whose work has appeared in the *Globe and Mail, Peterborough Examiner, Local Parent, Kawartha Cottage, Kawartha Homes, Our Canada,* and on CBC, Bravo Network, Rogers Television, TVOntario, and more. She grew up in Toronto and now lives in Peterborough, Ontario.